CAMPUS BOUND!

How to Choose
—and Get into—
the College That's
Right for You

BY ANNETTE SPENCE

PRICE STERN SLOAN

Los Angeles

A TERN ENTERPRISES BOOK

© 1990 by Tern Enterprises, Inc.

Published by Price Stern Sloan, Inc.
360 North La Cienega Boulevard,
Los Angeles, California 90048

Printed in the United States of America
9   8   7   6   5   4   3   2   1

LIBRARY OF CONGRESS CATALOGING-IN-PUBLICATION DATA
Spence, Annette.
     Campus bound! : how to choose and get into the college that's
right for you / by Annette Spence.
          p.   cm.
     ISBN 0-89586-773-7
     ISBN 0-89586-810-5 (pbk.)
     1. College, Choice of—United States.   2. Universities and
colleges—United States—Admission.   3. College student orientation—
-United States.   I. Title.
LB2350.5.S65   1989
378.1'056'0973—dc20   89-37530
                                                                   CIP

CAMPUS BOUND!
was prepared and produced by
Tern Enterprises, Inc.
15 West 26th Street
New York, New York 10010

Cover design: Virginia Rubel
Cover illustration: Dave Joly
Interior design: Judy Morgan
Interior illustrations: Joanna Roy

Maps on pages 54–55 reprinted by permission.

ACKNOWLEDGMENTS

Many thanks to:

The University of Tennessee at Knoxville. You weren't perfect, but you had "Rocky Top," the Pride of the Southland Marching Band, *The Daily Beacon* and journalism professor June Adamson.

Michele Rickman, undergraduate at Emory and Henry College and my real-life-college-student "consultant." You can go back to the library now, Michele. No more questions.

Newt Spence and Thelma Van Deman. They know why.

TABLE OF

C O N T E N T S

INTRODUCTION

Before I started writing this book, I never really thought about why I chose my college. Ever since I can remember, I knew that I would go to college. And ever since sixth grade—when I fell in love with *Gone With the Wind* and Margaret Mitchell—I knew that I would be a writer. But the decision about where to go to college to become a writer wasn't monumental. It just kind of happened.

Then I started reading college guides, interviewing college students and creating a step-by-step process for selecting a college. And in the middle of telephoning complete strangers in even stranger dormitories, I began to ask myself the same question I asked them: Why did I choose my college?

You want it straight? Because it had a decent journalism department. Because I was a flute player and it had a good marching band. Because it was two hours away from home, which was not too close and not too far away. Because it had an inexpensive, in-state tuition. Because I had a boyfriend there. And because I didn't know of many other options.

To be fair, my dad and I discussed a few other schools. When I was a high-school sophomore, we visited Tennessee Technological University, but the town of Cookeville seemed awfully boring and Tech didn't have a journalism department. East Tennessee State University was the most popular choice at my high school because it was thirty minutes away, inexpensive and easy to get into. But I didn't care for its proximity to my roots. (Even so, I applied to ETSU in case I wasn't accepted at my first-choice college.) Finally, my dad dreamed of sending me to the University of Missouri at Columbia, since he had heard about its prestigious journalism school. But every time we talked about it, he acted kind of nervous—I guess he was thinking about that out-of-state tuition. As for me, well, I didn't think I could handle the distance, and I wasn't that confident of my journalistic aptitude.

My parents were pleased with the college I chose, and to this day so am I. The journalism department wasn't the best in the country, but it gave me what I needed to get into the New York City publishing world. The marching band took me to the Bluebonnet Bowl in Houston and to President Reagan's 1980 inauguration in Washington, D.C. The tuition didn't break my dad's back and I managed to get home once a month to see Mom. And because my college also had a decent business school, I was fortunate enough to have my younger brother join me as an undergraduate.

Still, if I had to do it all over again, I wouldn't be so quick to choose. Who knows what the University of Missouri might have done for me? And if I had taken a shot at New York University, my entrance into New York City publishing might have been less painful. Then again, I'm not sure if either school would have accepted me. For me, this is water under the bridge, but you have the chance now to learn from the experience of others. Use this book to consider all your options: schools that excel in your field of study, schools that meet your religious requirements, schools that will put a stamp of prestige on your résumé forever. Then, if you decide to attend the college in your own backyard, at least you'll know you made the right choice at the time. And about ten years from now, when you reach the ripe old age of twenty-eight, as I have, you won't have to ask yourself why you chose your college. You'll know.

—*Annette Spence*
Class of 1983

P A R T   I

YOU'RE NOT IN KANSAS ANYMORE

Well, here you are. You've known this college thing was coming for a long time. Sometimes it seemed it would never get here, and sometimes you didn't care if it didn't. But it did, and now you're beginning to feel like Dorothy—or more like the cowardly lion. So now what?

First of all, relax. You've gotten this far, haven't you? Whether you realize it or not, getting through high school in one piece is not easy. So the fact that you're here, contemplating college, is something of a feat.

You may be wondering: Whose idea was this, anyway? Not only do you have to manage your schoolwork, but you've also got a busy social life (or at least you're working on one). And now you have to select a college, a major, a career! This is not at all like making plans for the weekend; you're making plans for your entire life.

Don't let this shake you up. The truth is, this is a big decision. But it's not one that will make or break you. Going to college, the right college, may open a lot of doors for you. Going to any college will influence your life for many years, perhaps forever. What you make of college—and the rest of your life, for that matter—is largely up to you. You can go to the most prestigious school in the country and mess yourself up with drugs or ignore your studies. Or you can go to some obscure community college and really make something of yourself by setting goals and working hard. In fact, you can bypass college completely and still be a success. The key is careful planning and discipline.

The discipline is something *you'll* have to provide, but you can get help with the planning right here. Planning is a series of decisions, and a decision like this is best made step by step. Once you examine all the avenues and take a good, long look at yourself, this college thing will be manageable and you'll feel more confident about making some choices. People have been making this decision for many years, and 99 percent of them lived through it. You will, too.

Warning: This might even be fun.

ARE YOU "RIGHT" FOR COLLEGE?

Don't ask yourself that. The first question you must answer is this: Is college right for you?

There are all too many cases of high-school students who (1) falsely believe they aren't "college material"; or (2) falsely believe they belong in college at all. It's true that college isn't for everyone, but you should make that decision based on what *you* want, not what you think others want.

Of course, there are other considerations that figure into the should-I or shouldn't-I question, such as your career goals and your likes and dislikes. Obviously, if books give you a rash or you're looking forward to a career in rock climbing, college may not be in your best interest. Let's try to frame the question a little more specifically....

A. Check any of the following statements that applies to you.

I'm thinking of going to college because...

- ☐ 1. I don't know what else to do.
- ☐ 2. I want freedom from my family and home.
- ☐ 3. I need a degree to pursue the career I want.
- ☐ 4. My parents want me to.
- ☐ 5. I want to meet new people.
- ☐ 6. I want to learn, to be educated.
- ☐ 7. All my friends are going.
- ☐ 8. It's fun.
- ☐ 9. I want to learn to be organized and think critically.
- ☐ 10. My parents will continue to support me.
- ☐ 11. I don't want to work yet.
- ☐ 12. I want to make a lot of money.
- ☐ 13. I want to be exposed to new ideas.
- ☐ 14. I want to participate in a fraternity, the marching band or some other club or extracurricular activity.
- ☐ 15. I want to see how I like it.
- ☐ 16. Everybody does.
- ☐ 17. I want to make a contribution to society.
- ☐ 18. I want to find out what I'm good at so I can choose a career.
- ☐ 19. I'm afraid not to.
- ☐ 20. It's free; I don't have to pay for it.

3

B. To interpret your responses, read the numbered paragraph that corresponds to the statements you checked.

1. Some people grow up knowing exactly what they want to do—go to college and get a job, get married and have kids, etc. Not everybody. There are plenty of people who turn forty without knowing what they want to do with themselves. The good news is you're not forty, so it's okay to feel unsure. But don't assume that college will give you all the answers. College

---

**FAMOUS AND SUCCESSFUL PEOPLE WHO WENT TO COLLEGE
(and Where They Went)***

Ronald Reagan	Eureka College—Eureka, Illinois
Alice Walker	Sarah Lawrence College—Bronxville, New York
Donald Trump	Wharton School of Finance at the University of Pennsylvania—Philadelphia, Pennsylvania
Julia Child	Smith College—Northampton, Massachusetts
Paul Newman	Kenyon College—Gambier, Ohio
Sally Ride	Stanford University—Stanford, California
Larry Bird	Indiana State University—Terre Haute, Indiana
Ed Bradley	Cheyney State College—Cheyney, Pennsylvania
Elizabeth Dole	Duke University—Durham, North Carolina
Lee Iacocca	Lehigh University—Bethlehem, Pennsylvania

*Includes completed undergraduate degrees only; some went on to graduate school elsewhere.

**FAMOUS AND SUCCESSFUL PEOPLE WHO DID NOT GO TO COLLEGE
(or at Least, Who Did Not Complete an Undergraduate Degree)**

David Brinkley	Richard Simmons
Frank Perdue	Andre Agassi
Michael Jackson	Charles Schulz
Cher	Hank Aaron
Peter Jennings	Estée Lauder

---

may give you some new ideas, but you have to look for them. Just being there isn't enough. If you like what college is all about—studying, socializing, learning how to be responsible— write "0" at the end of this paragraph. But if the idea of college seems to be rubbing you the wrong way, it may not be the best place for you to decipher your future. In that case, write "—" here. _____

2. This is only natural—though it shouldn't be the only reason you want to go to school. If you checked this box, write "0" here. _____

3. Good reasoning. If you checked off this box, write "+" here. _____

4. But what do *you* want? That's what's important. If you're thinking of college because your parents want you to, and you're not sure you want to, write "—" here. If you're going to college because that's what both you and your parents want, write "+" here. _____

5. Like most of the statements in part A, this shouldn't be the only reason you checked off. But it is a legitimate one. You will meet new people at college. At some colleges, the student body will be more diverse than at others. Later in this book we'll help you determine how important that variety is. For now, write "0" here. _____

6. Have you ever known someone who was "in love with being in love" and not necessarily "in love" with one person? Make sure that you're not in love with the idea of being educated. An undergraduate degree takes about four years to earn. To make it through those four years, you should be attracted to more than the distinction of being a college graduate. You should also be working toward a career goal, for example, or to amass knowledge on a particular subject. Write "+" if you genuinely like to learn. If you're not so sure, write "0" here. _____

7. Most high-school students admit that peers have a strong influence on their college-related decisions. Nevertheless, this is one situation in which you must separate your wants and needs from those of your friends. If you checked this box, write "—" here. _____

8. It *is* fun, for most people. But it goes without saying that there are more important reasons for attending college. If you checked this box, write "0" here. _____

9. You've got the right idea. In college you either learn to organize your time and work or you won't do well. Unlike high-school teachers, college profs let you do a lot of things on your own. They don't remind you that a test is coming up or tell you which points they make in class are the most important. As for learning to "think critically" or "think analytically," these are renowned liberal-arts-college goals. See page 46, *What About ...*, for more information. But first, write " + " here. _____

10. This is a common situation. Divorce contracts, insurance claims and family principles often dictate that children lose financial support upon high-school graduation unless they attend college. Think this one through. Do you want to go to college because you're not prepared to be on your own? If so, mark "—" here. _____

11. See number 10, above. Then mark "—" here. _____

12. The fact is, a college education and a high income do not necessarily go hand in hand. Ask any journalist or teacher. If money is your motive, take a step back. Investigate what jobs are most likely to pay well. Then find out what training or education is required. If college is part of the package, carry on. Mark "—" here if you don't have any career goals. But if you do have an inkling about what you wish to study in college, and you happen to know that it leads to a lucrative career (such as pre-med, engineering or accounting), write " + " here. _____

13. Tried-and-true reasoning. Be sure you know what "exposed to new ideas" means. Yes, college does give you the opportunity to meet new people, learn about new subjects and see yourself in a new light. Mark " + " here. _____

14. Think about what kind of organization you want to get involved in. Is it worthwhile? A group doesn't have to be stodgy and straight-and-narrow in order to be valuable. For example, some people look upon fraternities as if they exist purely for parties—but that's not always the case. Members may come away with experience in leadership and organizational skills and friendships that evolve into career contacts. Marching band, sports, newspaper staffs and the like have obvious benefits. And, of course, it's important to have fun, too. After you evaluate the group you'd like to join, mark " + " here if you think it's worthwhile, "0" here if it isn't. _____

15. If you think you have good reasons for going to college, but you're not sure it's your cup of tea, there's nothing wrong with going on a trial basis. As you read this book, you'll realize that this decision doesn't have to be the end of the world. How can we be 100 percent sure of everything all the time? Mark "0" here. ____

16. See number 7. Then mark "—" here. ____

17. What does this mean? Don't let catchy phrases confuse and mislead you. Get a grasp on what you want and need. Think about what contributing to society means to you. Social services? Art? Religion? Will college help you achieve this goal? The section on *What's Your Major?*, page 34, may help you decide. In the meantime, write "0" here. ____

18. Your reasoning is level-headed, but it's wise to find out as much as you can about yourself before you get to college. Although you'll take classes in a variety of subjects—especially during your first two years—these classes give you only basic information. That information may not be sufficient for you to make a career choice. However, if you have a general area of interest, college may help you narrow your scope. For example, if you're a good writer but don't know what to do with that talent, you might look into communications. As a communications major, you'll take classes in newspaper, radio, advertising and public relations. Chances are you'll find your niche. Mark " + " here. ____

19. Perhaps college is a "must" among your family and friends. Or maybe you don't have the nerve to tell your parents or teachers that you're not interested in college. There are better reasons for attending college. Mark "—" here. ____

20. It's tempting to attend college just because your tuition is provided for by scholarship, gift or financial aid. This is fine as long as you have other sound reasons for attending. Mark "0" here. ____

C. What do +, 0 and — mean? Record them in the space provided below, one under the other in the appropriate columns, and then we'll see how they stack up.

+	0	—
Strong reasons for attending	Secondary reasons for attending	Strong reasons against attending

When you finish, evaluate the chart. Which of the following best describes your response pattern?

• **Two or more +'s, some 0's, a minimum of —'s.**

College is more than likely a good choice for you. You have a genuine interest in what higher education has to offer. At the same time, you recognize that college has other benefits, such as friendship and independence. You're not overly concerned with the irrelevant reasons that frequently get in the way of a good decision. This book will help you put your interest to good use. Carry on.

• **Fewer than two +'s, the rest 0's and —'s.**

You're seriously considering college, but you need to make sure your motives will hold your interest through thick and thin. For now, you probably think it seems right to go mainly because you won a scholarship or because your parents really want you to. But do some soul searching before you decide. It will satisfy you personally to know that you're studying hard because you want to do something for yourself—not because it just happened. When you're fairly certain that college is right for you, this book will help you examine your college choices. What if it turns out you're not so certain? Consult your guidance counselor for alternatives; maybe he or she will suggest something that will click. In any case, don't give up on college yet. There are all kinds of schools that accommodate all kinds of needs. See *From Big Fish in a Little Pond* (page 42), and explore the *References* section (page 163) for books that might help.

• **A majority of —'s.**

Perhaps you're considering college to avoid something. Or maybe you have motives that weren't among the choices offered in section A. As it stands now, your answers indicate that college may not be your best bet. Not that you can't make the grade or won't fit in. But college isn't a way station for people who don't want to work or who don't know what to do. Talk to a guidance counselor about alternatives, such as the military, work-travel and apprenticeship programs. Or consider other types of schools: vocational, technical, nursing, art institutes (see *References*, page 167). Some students decide to delay going to college for a few months or years until they've tried something else or until they're sure college can offer what they want. And why not? Don't let yourself be rushed. It's been argued that the longer you wait, the harder it is to get back into the habit of studying. It's also been observed that the longer you wait, the more discipline you have and the more you appreciate learning.

WORDS OF WISDOM

"The worst possible approach toward college is to think of it as something being pushed on you by your parents, professors or 'society'. . . . Instead of seeing yourself at the mercy of forces acting upon you, just doing what other people want you to do, you can see yourself as the director of your own future. You can take charge and make your own choices."

—Marcia K. Johnson, Sally P. Springer and Sarah Hall Sternglanz
How to Succeed in College

Where Does This Leave You?

Only you can decide if college is right for you. Obviously, a quiz in a book cannot determine your future; rather, it is designed to give you insight and perspective, to make you think. What if you think you know what's right, but you can't be too sure?

You're not going to like this, but life is a lot like that. When you get married, change jobs or buy a house, you can be positive only to a point, and then you just have to trust your instincts. Not to worry. If you've thought through the situation and weighed the options, you're probably doing right. Things usually work out for the best.

THE TYPICAL COLLEGE SEARCH: WHY DOESN'T IT WORK?

About six of every ten high-school graduates enroll in college. Of those students, about 75 percent say they are attending their first-choice college, and approximately 20 percent end up with

Why I Chose Brown University
—Providence, Rhode Island

"Brown University was a popular choice among the seniors at my high school in Carlisle, Massachusetts. Its academic reputation was excellent. The students at Brown were said to be a diverse, creative and independent group. The university-size curriculum included progressive new programs in semiotics and women's studies, while the campus had the friendly feel of a small college.

"These things were important to me. I wanted to go to a good school but not a snob school. I felt I could make a place for myself at Brown and pursue my interest in the studio arts, while sampling other courses in the humanities. Brown's exchange program with the Rhode Island School of Design [RISD] was also attractive. And I liked the fact that Brown had no core curriculum; I felt I had earned the right to forgo science and math.

"I never did take any classes at RISD. And while I could have used more guidance in choosing my courses during the first two years, I have never regretted choosing Brown. I'm grateful that Brown chose me—and offered me a good financial-aid package. I'm glad that my friends and teachers at Brown encouraged me to think independently and find my own way, even if it sometimes meant learning from my own mistakes."

Sara Donovan Whitford
Class of 1981
Freelance Art Director
Boston, MA

their second choice. Even so, about half of these college-bound students say that when they actually made their decisions about where to go, they didn't have enough information. Thus, they still weren't sure they'd made the right choices. How can this be?

There are a few compelling reasons. The first is the over-whelming amount of information available on colleges. Book-stores and libraries are well stocked with college guides. College administrators themselves mail out scores of catalogs and brochures. Advertising, media attention and marketing schemes contribute their own brands of hype. Thus, it becomes difficult to figure out what information sources to read or disregard, trust or scrutinize. No wonder high-school students and parents get confused!

The process is also hindered by distance. A campus visit is highly recommended, but that's not always possible, especially for out-of-staters. Consequently, some students choose schools without seeing them—or, even more likely, drop long-distance prospects from their lists, which is a shame.

Finally, the typical college search doesn't work because there is no method to the madness. Students don't know how to go about making the decision or where to turn for answers. Guidance counselors? They do the best they can, but they're busy. The National Association of College Admission Coun-selors estimates that the typical counselor tends to 400 stu-dents, and in some schools as many as 1,000. New on the scene are private counselors who aim to take the load off the high-school help and make a buck at the same time. Whether or not they're succeeding is not yet clear, but one thing's certain: Right now, private counselors are only adding fuel to the fire of confusion (see *Does Private Advice Pay?*, page 100).

It's a jungle out there, all right. This book is designed to help. You won't find any hundred-dollar bills to finance a trip to the University of Hawaii, but you will find suggestions for handling the long-distance problem (see page 116). And you won't find a substitute for the personal attention of your guidance counselor, but you will find step-by-step guidance for making your deci-sion.

SO WHERE DO YOU START?

That all depends on where you are now. Here's the basic plan of action.

If you're a freshman or sophomore, you have a good amount of time to spend researching colleges and planning for your junior and senior years:

• Take every opportunity to talk to college students, alumni and teachers. Ask questions.

• Visit college campuses whenever you have the chance—for football games or seminars, for example. You don't have to be interested in the school; seeing *any* campus will give you a point of reference.

• Read newspaper and magazine articles about colleges and the college search. Books help, too.

• Read any campus publications—catalogs, newspapers, magazines, brochures—that cross your path.

• Attend "college nights."

• Pay attention to what you like and what you're good at. Think about how you might shape those skills and talents into a career.

• Talk to people whose jobs interest you. Ask what education paths they took.

• Keep your grades up throughout your high-school career. Don't wait until your senior year.

• Participate. Extracurricular activities—such as student council, sports and clubs—will look good on your application.

• Choose your classes wisely (see *Stay the Course,* page 67). Strive to improve your writing and studying skills.

• Take the PSAT (Preliminary Scholastic Aptitude Test) in your sophomore year if you have the opportunity.

If you're a junior, you'll want to get right to work. In addition to the suggestions for freshmen and sophomores, here's what you should do:

• Make an appointment with your guidance counselor. Talk about your college preparation and your personal interests.

• Sign up for and take the PSAT (Preliminary Scholastic Aptitude Test), if you haven't already. Your counselor will give you the dates of the exam. (Some kids take it twice. See page 15 for test information.)

• Develop a list of potential schools.

• Begin to write to colleges for catalogs, financial-aid forms and applications.

• Visit schools in which you're interested.

• Keep your ear to the ground for scholarship possibilities.

• Take the SAT (Scholastic Aptitude Test) and ACT (American College Test) in the spring if: (1) your counselor advises it; (2) you think you may be an Early Decision or Early Action candidate; or (3) you are graduating early.

• Find out your class rank and grade-point average—it will be necessary for applications and it may help you determine what colleges you should consider.

If you're a senior, you've probably already taken some of the steps outlined above. Hurry and catch up, because you have to:

• Write to colleges for catalogs, financial-aid information and applications (if you haven't done so already).

• Make arrangements for college interviews, if necessary.

• Sign up for and take your SAT and ACT tests in the fall, if you haven't already.

• Visit more college campuses.

• See college representatives who come to your high school.

• Ask teachers or alumni for letters of recommendation, if necessary.

• Narrow your list of schools to about two to five choices.

• Complete and mail school applications.

• Complete and mail financial-aid forms.

• Reply to colleges that offer admissions.

• Notify a college of your decision to enroll.

• Accommodate any requests your accepted college may have (deposits, information, orientations).

• Complete your high-school work and graduate.

• Line up a summer job and get ready for September.

WHAT HAVE YOU ACCOMPLISHED?

Check off the steps you've already taken. Leave blank the ones you haven't.

- ☐ Visited some campuses
- ☐ Attended college nights
- ☐ Met with your guidance counselor
- ☐ Looked at college catalogs at school or in the library
- ☐ Talked to alumni and college students about schools
- ☐ Talked to workers about their jobs
- ☐ Learned about some scholarships
- ☐ Signed up for the PSAT
- ☐ Completed the PSAT
- ☐ Requested catalogs, applications and financial-aid forms
- ☐ Signed up for the SAT
- ☐ Completed the SAT
- ☐ Signed up for the ACT
- ☐ Completed the ACT
- ☐ Asked teachers or alumni for letters of recommendation (optional)
- ☐ Applied for Early Decision (optional)
- ☐ Completed and mailed financial-aid applications
- ☐ Gathered scholarship applications
- ☐ Completed and mailed scholarship applications
- ☐ Mailed your senior-year mid-term grades to your chosen colleges
- ☐ Gathered college applications
- ☐ Completed and mailed applications

The preceding list isn't complete—and you're not expected to check off all the boxes. (If you did, you don't need this book!) The list is simply supposed to point out the events and goals you'll want to schedule on your *College-Search Timetable*.

But First, a Word About Tests

Students interested in college usually take the *Preliminary Scholastic Aptitude Test/National Merit Scholarship Qualifying Test* in October of their junior year, sometimes in their sophomore year. This test score won't be submitted with your college applications, but it might qualify you for a scholarship or award. It will also give you a hint of what the SAT is like. Your guidance counselor's office will have information on the test, which will be administered somewhere in your area, probably at your own school. When you sign up, ask for a free copy of the *PSAT/NMSQT Student Bulletin*, which contains a practice test prepared by the College Entrance Examination Board, the organization that coordinates the test.

Between the spring of your junior year and fall of your senior year, you'll probably take the *Scholastic Aptitude Test*. Most colleges require or accept the SAT, so you should take the test even if you're not sure you'll need it. The College Entrance Examination Board permits you to take the SAT up to three times. Colleges accept the most recent score, an average of your scores or your highest score. When you sign up, ask for a free copy of *Taking the SAT*, which contains a sample exam.

The American College Test is also required by many schools, either in addition to, or instead of, the SAT. Some scholarships use ACT scores for the selection process, too. Like the SAT, most students take it between the spring of their junior year and fall of their senior year. Unlike the SAT, however, the ACT is ordinarily taken only once. The ACT is coordinated by the American College Testing Program.

The more selective colleges may also require or recommend *College Board Achievement Tests*, which measure your performance in a specific subject. For example, the California Institute of Technology, in Pasadena, requires tests in English composition, math and either physics, biology or chemistry. Earlham College in Richmond, Indiana, recommends two tests in essays, creative work or academic projects. If you excel in a particular subject or if you're certain you'll compete for spots in the most selective schools, see your counselor about these tests.

You'll take them at various times during the year. Get *About the Achievement Tests* from your counselor, or write to the College Entrance Examination Board (see *References,* page 166, for the address).

Unfortunately, a few colleges place too much importance on these test scores—consequently, students put too much pressure on themselves to do well. Some administrators prefer to put emphasis on your overall high-school performance. But it wouldn't hurt for you to study the booklets that prepare you for these tests. Also available are preparatory books and computer programs. Check the library, bookstore or software store. (Some titles are listed in *References,* pages 165–166 and 170–171.)

And a Word About Early Decisions

Your College-Search Timetable is influenced by many variables:

Regular Admissions. The majority of students take their college-preparatory tests in the fall of their senior year and then follow a "Regular Admissions" deadline. This means they submit their applications and financial-aid forms in the winter and receive acceptance notices in the spring. However, your schedule will be different under the following circumstances.

Early Action. You'll come across this term in all college-search literature (but not all schools have this program). Schools with this admissions program allow you to apply at an earlier date (usually in the fall) than the regular deadline in winter. In return, you get an early notification (or denial) of your acceptance. If you get an Early Action acceptance, you are not obliged to attend the college. You might consider applying by Early Action if you'd like to attend a particular school but aren't sure you can get in. Only strong applicants are admitted—others are transferred to the general application pool.

Early Decision. Like Early Action, an Early Decision permits you to apply before the regular deadline and receive a verdict ahead of time. The difference between the two: With Early Decision, you are obligated to accept no other college. You should apply for Early Decision only if you're sure you want to attend a particular school.

Rolling Admission. Schools with this kind of program accept students until they fill the upcoming freshman class. In some cases, one early deadline is set up. For example, the University of Southern Florida begins to consider applications on July 1, the summer preceding your senior year. Other schools, such as the Illinois Institute of Technology, set up two or three dates. Obviously, with Rolling Admission schools, you want to get your application in as soon as possible.

HOW TO USE YOUR COLLEGE-SEARCH TIMETABLE

1. Decide if you're a candidate for Early Action or Early Decision. If you're already interested in a few schools, it wouldn't hurt to check their admissions program now. Go to the library or your guidance counselor's office and look in the college catalogs or one of the college guides, such as *The Right College* or *Peterson's Guide to Colleges*. If any of them has an admissions program that requires you to submit an application in the summer before or fall of your senior year, plan your Timetable accordingly.

2. Take another look at the sections *So Where Do You Start?* and *What Have You Accomplished?* Then plot these goals and events on the Timetable.

3. Refer to and update the Timetable throughout your search.

COLLEGE-SEARCH TIMETABLE

Freshman Year

Goals

1. Visit Tennessee Tech in Cookeville
2.
3.
4.
5.
6.
7.
8.
9.
10.

Events

1. College Night on September 20
2.
3.
4.
5.
6.
7.
8.
9.
10.

COLLEGE - SEARCH TIMETABLE

Sophomore Year

Goals

1. Take PSAT
2.
3.
4.
5.
6.
7.
8.
9.
10.

Events

1. Oct. 14, PSAT at Sullivan Central High, 9 A.M.
2.
3.
4.
5.
6.
7.
8.
9.
10.

COLLEGE-SEARCH TIMETABLE

Fall, Junior Year

Goals

1.

2.

3.

4.

5.

6.

7.

8.

9.

10.

Events

1.

2.

3.

4.

5.

6.

7.

8.

9.

10.

REMINDERS:

- Make sure you take the PSAT.
- Take advantage of college nights.
- Attend college football games—the perfect opportunity to visit campuses.
- Select courses that will improve your application: literature, advanced math and science, foreign languages.

COLLEGE-SEARCH TIMETABLE

Winter, Junior Year

Goals

1.
2.
3.
4.
5.
6.
7.
8.
9.
10.

Events

1.
2.
3.
4.
5.
6.
7.
8.
9.
10.

REMINDERS:

• PSAT results come in December for students who took it in October.
• Early decision/action candidates: Schedule SAT and ACT for spring.
• Keep asking questions of college students and alumni.
• Make good grades.

COLLEGE-SEARCH TIMETABLE

Spring, Junior Year

Goals

1.

2.

3.

4.

5.

6.

7.

8.

9.

10.

Events

1.

2.

3.

4.

5.

6.

7.

8.

9.

10.

REMINDERS:

• Early decision/action candidates: Complete applications by June.

• Write for catalogs.

• Find out if any schools from your preliminary list require on-campus interviews.

• Find out your grade-point average and class rank.

• Choose your senior courses wisely.

COLLEGE-SEARCH TIMETABLE

Summer, Junior Year

Goals

1.

2.

3.

4.

5.

6.

7.

8.

9.

10.

Events

1.

2.

3.

4.

5.

6.

7.

8.

9.

10.

REMINDERS:

• Work and save money for college.
• At some schools, Early or Rolling Admissions applications are due.
• Plan campus visits around vacations.

23

COLLEGE-SEARCH TIMETABLE

Fall, Senior Year

Goals

1.

2.

3.

4.

5.

6.

7.

8.

9.

10.

Events

1.

2.

3.

4.

5.

6.

7.

8.

9.

10.

REMINDERS:

• Most students take the SAT and ACT now.

• Contact teachers who are writing letters of recommendation for you.

• At some schools, Early or Rolling Admissions applications are due.

• Meet college representatives who may come to your school.

• Attend college football games!

• Keep studying and making good grades.

COLLEGE-SEARCH TIMETABLE

Winter, Senior Year

Goals

1.

2.

3.

4.

5.

6.

7.

8.

9.

10.

Events

1.

2.

3.

4.

5.

6.

7.

8.

9.

10.

REMINDERS:

• Most applications are due now.

• Financial-aid forms are also due.

• If you haven't taken the SAT or ACT, schedule it now.

• Some colleges require your mid-year grades now.

COLLEGE-SEARCH TIMETABLE

Spring, Senior Year

Goals

1.
2.
3.
4.
5.
6.
7.
8.
9.
10.

Events

1.
2.
3.
4.
5.
6.
7.
8.
9.
10.

REMINDERS:

- The admission verdicts begin to come in.
- This is your last chance to take the SAT.
- It's time to make final college decisions.
- Some colleges require deposits now.
- Look into scholarships and other financial aid.

C O L L E G E - S E A R C H T I M E T A B L E

Summer, Senior Year

Goals

1.

2.

3.

4.

5.

6.

7.

8.

9.

10.

Events

1.

2.

3.

4.

5.

6.

7.

8.

9.

10.

REMINDERS:
- Graduate!
- Work for school money.
- Gather the things you'll need for college.
- Attend orientation.
- Pat yourself on the back.

Why I Chose the University of North Carolina-Chapel Hill
—Chapel Hill, North Carolina

"When I was in tenth grade, our high-school drama club went to the University of North Carolina to perform in the state theater festival. Although I grew up near Sanford, North Carolina, this was really the first time I had ever seen the campus and visited the town. I had never considered going to college before, but I really liked Chapel Hill and the people in the drama department. Then, the next year, I got a small part in an outdoor drama by Paul Green, The Highland Call. Paul Green was a Pulitzer-Prize-winner who went to UNC and who grew up on a farm, as I had. All the major actors in the drama were either affiliated with the university or from Chapel Hill, and that's when I decided I had to go there—I didn't consider any other school.

"My family couldn't afford my full tuition, so I worked summers and got assistantships, loans and scholarships. When I did an assistantship in theater publicity, I became interested in writing. I decided to take some journalism courses in my junior year, and I got pretty good at it.

"I graduated with a B.A. in dramatic arts and went on to graduate school in the drama department. I thought about being a theatrical press agent, but then I started to get acting jobs. I played in a number of national touring productions, among them The Great White Hope and Barefoot in the Park (in which I had the lead). In between acting jobs, I worked at a New York City public relations company and I began to see writing and theatrical flair as a perfect combination. After five years of supporting myself as a professional actor, I decided to go with public relations as a career.

"I wouldn't change anything about my college choice. It broadened my horizons and I met people from a lot of different backgrounds—people that I'm still friends with today. And of course, working in theater, having to analyze characters, I came to appreciate differences in people more. So in addition to a good education, UNC gave me an appreciation of people and ideas and culture that I had never been exposed to before. It helped develop me not just intellectually, but also as a person with diverse interests and concerns."

—Gordon Clark
Class of 1961
Vice President
The Rowland Company
New York, NY

WHAT COULD GO WRONG?

Nothing you can't handle. Here are some problems that could occur over the next months:

• Information Overload

Applications, transcripts, brochures, essay notes—the amount of material you're dealing with is enough to drive anybody over the edge. Don't let it get to you. Instead, *organize*. Use the quizzes and worksheets in this book to organize your thoughts and plans. If we've missed anything, start your own looseleaf notebook or composition book of college information. Store your applications and other paraphernalia in folders or large envelopes. Or, consider sending away for *The College Admissions Organizer*, a big notebook of pockets designed to store your information and record your progress (see *References,* page 165, for ordering information).

• Parental Pressure

They mean no harm. Some parents simply get over-involved because: (1) they want you to do what they did; (2) they want you to do what they didn't do; (3) they think you need help; and so

on. You may very well need their help—especially with financial-aid forms, campus visits and money. But the time may come when you need space to make your decision and do what it takes to get in. Talk to your parents; tell them you're glad they're showing so much interest but that now's the time for you to assert your independence and start taking responsibility. That's partly what going to college is about, anyway.

• **Panic Attack**

It may be caused by Information Overload, Parental Pressure or any number of the moving pieces in the College-Search Game. Try to prevent panic by organizing your search and staying on top of all the deadlines. If you get shaky anyway, talk it out with someone who makes you feel good—your family, friends or teachers. You'll get some of the stress off your chest and they'll reassure you. Be nice to yourself, too. Get out for a movie, a new haircut, a game of basketball. Don't underestimate the power of laughing with your friends or working up a good sweat—both humor and exercise are proven stress-relievers.

P A R T   I I

HAPPY HUNTING

You *could* just grab the tiger by the tail, apply to the first three or four colleges that come to mind and then sit back and let nature take its course. Or you could take some time to think about what's really important to the college search, develop a "pool of schools" to choose from and then proceed with the application process. Let's do it that way. Who knows? You may eventually choose the college next door. But by taking it easy, step by step, you'll get your priorities straightened out and feel more confident about your decisions.

First, consider your field of study. It could have everything to do with which schools are right and which schools are wrong. A student in agriculture, for example, would be wise to choose the University of California at Davis over the Saint Paul Seminary. The section called *What's Your Major?* (page 34) will help you examine this guiding principle.

From Big Fish in a Little Pond (page 42) is about choosing the type of school you think is right: Big? Small? Specialized? Military? There's something for everybody.

Location is another big deciding factor. *Absence Makes the Heart Grow Fonder* (page 48) helps you determine whether you're a homebody or a free spirit, and whether you're more suited for New York City or Northfield, Minnesota.

And finally, *The Other Things* (page 56) gives you a chance to speak out about social life, prestige, extracurricular activities, parents—factors that shouldn't dictate your college decision, but which are nevertheless influential.

What about being able to afford certain schools, not having the grades, a college's academic credentials and the like? We'll get to that. Once you take a good look at field of study, type of school, location and the other things, you'll assemble a "pool of schools." Then you can get down to the nitty-gritty of financial aid, accreditation and selectivity. Through a process of elimination, you'll arrive at the best colleges to apply to.

The reasoning *behind* this procedure is to get you to indulge—to study yourself, your college wants and your college needs. Prospective college students are notorious for selling themselves short, for not taking chances. Okay, so maybe Harvard *is* a little out of your grade range. But don't knock it until you've tried. If you've got a hankering to graduate from one of the "greats," put it in your pool of schools, and then look into it. You might be able to squeeze in. Or a scholarship could land in your lap.

Start Now!

Begin writing away for college catalogs. Although you can find copies in your guidance counselor's office or in the public library, the selection may be localized and out of date. Not all colleges will send the actual catalog in the first mailing (too expensive), but they will send a packet of information including brochures, an application, financial-aid information and a reply card. When you get ready to whittle down your pool of schools, these packets will help immensely. Of course, you should write to the schools that interest you most, but it doesn't hurt to write to others as well. This way, you'll be able to compare.

How do you do all this? Go to the library or your guidance counselor's office. Ask for one of the college guides—most of them include college addresses (see *References,* page 163, for the names of some guides). Send a postcard to the Admissions Office requesting additional information. Don't forget to include your address. Store all of the information you receive in a file or a box. You might even want to keep a log that looks something like this:

C A T A L O G   L I S T

	Available at library/office?	Sent for	Received
Example: Univ. of Mo. at Columbia	No	11/30/90	1/2/91
1.			
2.			
3.			
4.			
5.			
6.			
7.			
8.			
9.			
10.			

WHAT'S YOUR MAJOR?

There are three kinds of college students:

- **The "I've-Always-Known-What-I-Want-to-Do."**

This kind of high-school student has known since sixth grade that he or she is destined to be a dancer/doctor/designer, as the case may be. This person is most likely to know where he or she wants to go to college, too. This causes unpopularity among the other two kinds of students, and, consequently, he or she has a shorter life expectancy.

- **The "I've-Got-a-Hunch-But-I'm-Not Sure."**

The high-school student of this nature has displayed talent in a general area and has surmised that he or she may have found her calling. However, the typical "I've-Got-a-Hunch" is practical. He or she suspects that winning a grade-school chemistry badge in 1980 does not a chemist make.

- **The "Beats Me."**

He or she doesn't have an inkling of how to spend the next fifty years. "I'll know it when I see it," he or she says. Which is unlikely since, in the past year, he or she has seen very little except the *Nightmare on Elm Street* movies and their creepy cousins.

Welcome to the world of *What's Your Major?* Few of us fit into the "I've-Always-Known" category, but the people who do will have a leg up on the competition. If history is your strength, for example, you'd look into schools with strong history departments, such as Reed College, in Portland, Oregon. Interested in dentistry? Then maybe Tufts University, in Medford, Massachusetts, is right for you.

Nobody says you have to decide on your major today. It's hard to be sure about something this important (especially if you haven't been thinking about it since sixth grade). In fact, some colleges encourage freshman *not* to choose a major—at least not until they've had a sampling of liberal-arts courses. For now, your goal is finding a field of study. Then you can:

Explore various careers within your major. For example, as a student of economics, your career choices range from marketing research to insurance underwriting. As you get to know more about economics, the possibilities will present themselves. Then you can find out which branch pays you the most, gives you the most power, satisfaction or recognition—whatever your career goals may be.

Think and learn. Not all students go to college to develop a career. Many go for the sake of knowledge itself—career choice comes later. If this is your goal, you can be less concerned about whether your field of study leads to a career.

WHERE THE JOBS ARE

It's good to find an area of study and career in which you excel and that you enjoy. It's even better to find a field that also has a bright future! According to the United States Department of Labor, here are the ten fastest-growing occupations through the year 2000.

1. Paralegal
2. Medical Assistant
3. Physical Therapist
4. Home Health Aide
5. Podiatrist
6. Computer Systems Analyst
7. Employment Interviewer
8. Computer Programmer
9. Dental Hygienist
10. Physician Assistant

Change your mind. Let's say you always thought you had the hands, mind and soul of a musician. So you decided to major in music. But after two months of drawing treble clefs and singing scales, you know you've made a mistake. Better now than later. It was an experiment, and a good one at that. Now all you have to do is change your major.

If you're an "I've-Always-Known," you're in luck. Just be sure that you don't close too many doors too soon. Now's the time to explore the possibilities. Don't rule out your fascination with computer science simply because you've been told you're a natural-born actor.

The same thing holds true if you're an "I've-Got-a-Hunch." Don't settle on a major until you've toyed with a few other ideas. Think you'd like to go into accounting? Good, but if there are other areas in the business field that spark your interest—management or finance, for example—don't dedicate yourself to accounting.

If you're a "Beats Me," you've got some research to do. In addition to taking the mini-questionnaire that follows, consider a full-scale test that measures your aptitude in various fields of study. Your guidance counselor should know where such tests are available—they're usually given at local colleges. Two books may also be of help: *What Color Is Your Parachute?*, by Richard Nelson Bolles; and *Do What You Love—The Money Will Follow: Discovering Your Right Livelihood*, by Marsha Sinetar. These are available in most bookstores. (See *References*, page 166, for more details.)

This mini-questionnaire may reveal things about your personal likes, dislikes, skills and whatnot that might help you choose a field of study.

THINGS YOU LIKE TO DO

Hobbies

1.   2.

3.   4.

Schoolwork

1.   2.

3.   4.

Extracurricular Activities

1.   2.

3.   4.

Community/Religion

1.   2.

3.   4.

Pastimes

1.   2.

3.   4.

Choose four of the activities you listed above and explain why you like them.

1.   2.

3.   4.

THINGS AT WHICH YOU'RE GOOD

School

1.   2.

3.   4.

Home

Examples: Baby-Sitting, Gardening, Car Maintenance, Organizing

1.   2.

3.   4.

Other

Examples: Your Part-Time Job, Planning Parties, Hobbies

1.   2.

3.   4.

Analyze what makes you good at four of these activities.

1.   2.

3.   4.

Careers/Areas of Study That Seem to Fit You

What have you always thought about being or doing? In what fields can you imagine yourself? What careers really interest you?

1.

2.

3.

4.

5.

6.

7.

8.

9.

10.

College Majors That Might Interest You*

Keeping in mind all that you've written above, read the following list of major fields of study. Do any of the descriptives ring a bell? If so check the appropriate box. Remember that there are many branches in each general field of study—we've given only a few examples for each heading.

☐ Agriculture
  Farm management; fish, game and wildlife management; forestry; agricultural business
☐ Architecture
  Building design, landscape design, city and community planning
☐ Biological Sciences
  Anatomy, botany, environmental science, zoology

*Source: *Index of Majors* (see *References,* page 168).

☐ Business and Management
Accounting, marketing, insurance, real estate, hotel and restaurant management

☐ Communications
Advertising, journalism, radio and television

☐ Computer Science
Computer programming, data processing, systems analysis

☐ Education
Physical education, junior-high-school education, special education

☐ Engineering
Nuclear engineering, chemical engineering, mechanical engineering

☐ Fine Arts
Dance, art history, cinematography, music theory, sculpture

☐ Foreign Languages
Arabic, Latin, German, Japanese, Italian

☐ Health Professions
Medicine, pharmacy, dentistry, optometry, speech pathology

☐ Law
General law, criminal justice, pre-law

☐ Letters
English literature, philosophy, creative writing

☐ Physical Sciences
Astronomy, geology, oceanography, physics, chemistry

☐ Psychology
Clinical psychology, social psychology, psychology for counseling

☐ Social Sciences
Anthropology, economics, geography, history, sociology

☐ Theology
Religious education, religious music, theological professional (rabbi, minister)

Why I Chose the University of California-Berkeley
—Berkeley, California

"I was fourteen years old when I wrote an essay that said, 'When I grow up, I'm going to the University of California at Berkeley because those who don't wish they did.' Most of my friends went to UCLA, which is close to my childhood home in southern California. But in my mind, Berkeley was the finest school in California. My parents went there, my brothers went there, and I had to go, too. As it happened, I not only completed my undergraduate degree in biology, I also earned my Ph.D. in anatomy at Berkeley. I was fascinated to learn how integrated systems worked, such as the nervous, endocrine and cardiovascular systems. The brain attracted me the most and I've been studying it ever since.

"Looking back—after twenty-five years as a professor here—I am still convinced that I made the right choice. There is such a diversity here; the imagination is your only limitation. If I get an idea there is always someone on campus who I can relate to, who can help me move ahead. For example, yesterday the researchers at Lawrence Berkeley lab got the super-conductor magnet up to nine Tesla for the first time. They called and asked if we wanted to put our little rats in one of those big, powerful magnetic fields. We were there just as fast as we could get there, because knowledge gained from such magnets will aid in future studies when higher magnetic fields are used for imaging human brains."

—Dr. Marian Cleeves Diamond
Class of 1948 (undergraduate)
Professor of Anatomy
Author of *Enriching Heredity: The Impact of the
Environment on the Anatomy of the Brain* (1988)
Berkeley, CA

FROM BIG FISH IN A LITTLE POND...

...to little fish in a big pond. That's how some students describe the transition from senior in high school to freshman in college. But this doesn't have to be the case—when it comes to college, one size doesn't fit all. To help determine whether a large or small school is right for you, work through the following exercise. Once you've reached an answer, use that criterion to help you choose your college.

Check any of the following statements that apply:

Large Colleges

☐ I like my independence. I prefer going to a school where everyone doesn't know me, where I can "start over."

☐ I like seeing different faces. Having different instructors, meeting new people whenever I change classes or dormitories—that appeals to me.

☐ I like variety. It's important to me to have a lot of campus activities—movies, concerts, athletic facilities—from which to choose.

☐ I like selection. I don't want my choice of courses or instructors to be limited.

☐ I like opportunities. I'm not sure of my interests yet, so I need a college that offers me information on many fields of study.

☐ I like traditional big-college activities. Football games, fraternities and sororities, marching bands and the like are important to me.

Small Colleges

☐ I like familiarity. I want to feel as if I belong to a community of students instead of a city of students.

☐ I like attention. I want my instructors to know who I am and how I'm doing.

☐ I don't like competition. I want to enroll in classes and dormitories and participate in activities with ease.

☐ I like informality. I prefer an easygoing environment to an orderly one.

☐ I like to concentrate. Extracurricular and campus activities do not appeal to me and they distract from my studies.

☐ I like specialization. I'm fairly sure of my field of study and do not feel the need to be in a school that offers a wide selection.

KEEP IN MIND:

• A large school enrolls more than 10,000 students. Examples are Northwestern University (10,400), in Evanston, Illinois, and the University of Minnesota at Minneapolis (44,300).

• A small school enrolls fewer than 4,000 students. Examples are Bradford College (430), in Bradford, Massachusetts, and Brandeis University (3,700), in Waltham, Massachusetts.

• Not all large colleges are impersonal, and not all small colleges are limited. Before you rule out a great school that otherwise just isn't your ideal size, do some research. Read *The Fiske Guide to Colleges* or *Insider's Guide to the Colleges* (see *References,* page 164) to see if the institution fits a stereotype. Or turn to page 116, *The Fine Art of Asking Questions,* and get the scoop yourself.

Should you consider a women's college? A two-year program? Check any of the following statements that apply to you.

Two-Year Colleges

☐ I have very little money to put into a college education.

☐ I have to live at home, and there are no four-year universities or colleges nearby.

☐ I'm not sure I'm ready for four years of college.

☐ I'm sure my grades aren't good enough for college.

KEEP IN MIND:

• Two-year colleges, also known as junior or community colleges, have different kinds of programs. Some require only two years of school and provide an "associate's degree" or "certificate" in real estate, secretarial science, mechanical designing—whatever the case may be. One kind of program is transferable; after two years at a junior college, you may be able to enter a four-year college as a junior. Check with the admissions office of the two-year school you're considering—as well as the four-year school you'll transfer to—to see how this works.

• Public junior colleges are tax-supported and are usually required to accept high-school graduates of the district or state, regardless of grades.

• Private junior colleges are usually administered by religious or other independent groups. Their students are more likely to come from outside the community.

• Two-year schools are generally less expensive because they don't require as much expensive equipment or buildings as four-year schools, some are tax-supported and some enable you to live at home.

Women's Colleges

☐ I'm majoring in a career that is traditionally male-dominated, and I want to avoid any discrimination.

☐ By attending all-female classes, I can concentrate better—I need help in separating my academic life from my social life.

☐ I'd like the chance to perform in an all-female student body.

☐ I'm interested in feminism, and a women's college would provide a unique opportunity for me to learn more.

☐ I don't mind going off campus to meet men.

KEEP IN MIND:

• Only a few women's colleges remain. You can find a list in *Peterson's National College Databank* (see *References,* page 168).

• There are pros and cons for attending a women's college. Before you assume that a stereotype is true, visit the campus.

Black Colleges

- ☐ I prefer to attend classes and participate in social activities with black students.
- ☐ I prefer a small college (black schools usually are).
- ☐ I am black, and I am concerned about discrimination in a predominantly white college.
- ☐ I am interested in civil rights, and attending a black college would provide a unique opportunity to learn more.

KEEP IN MIND:

- Only 107 predominantly black colleges remain. Most are private. For a list, see *Peterson's National College Databank.*
- There are also pros and cons for attending black colleges. For more information, see *The Black Student's Guide to College* (see *References,* page 164).

Military Colleges/Service Academies

- ☐ I am interested in military science.
- ☐ I like studying and living in an environment of discipline and order.
- ☐ I enjoy physical activity.
- ☐ I handle stress well.
- ☐ I can be a follower as well as a leader.

KEEP IN MIND:

- The service academies—such as the U.S. Military Academy at West Point and the U.S. Naval Academy at Annapolis—are among the most competitive of institutions. However, the government pays educational expenses and a salary to accepted students.
- Other military colleges, such as The Citadel, in Charleston, South Carolina, and Virginia Military Institute, in Lexington, Virginia, are not as demanding, but are nevertheless competitive.
- The process and timetable for applying to the service academies differs. For information, see *References,* page 167.

Specialized Colleges

- ☐ I am sure about what field I want to study.
- ☐ I think I will get the best education for my field in a specialized college.
- ☐ I prefer to associate with people who have the same career interests; I don't feel the need to attend classes with students in various fields of study.
- ☐ I am not interested in traditional college activities, such as athletic events and social fraternities.

KEEP IN MIND:

• As always, it's best to visit the campus before assuming anything about its personality.

• Specializations range from aviation (Embry-Riddle Aeronautical University) to veterinary science (Bel-Rea Institute of Animal Technology). Consult a college guide or *Peterson's National College Databank* for examples.

Denominational Colleges

- ☐ I want religion to be part of my daily life.
- ☐ I want to go to school with students of my own religious background.
- ☐ I want to take advantage of the education my religious group supports.
- ☐ I want to show my support for my religion.

KEEP IN MIND:

• The level of religious influence in a denominational institution varies. For example, at Baylor University, in Waco, Texas, students are required to take religion courses and the social climate is tempered by a Baptist administration. On the other hand, Georgetown University, in Washington, D.C., is purportedly very "unCatholiclike." Visit, ask questions and see for yourself.

What About . . .

Private vs. Public Schools?

The myth is that private colleges are more expensive than public ones, but that's not necessarily true. Because they wish to attract students from all sorts of financial backgrounds, most private schools offer some good financial-aid packages. The main difference between private and public institutions is that the former are supported by non-government interests, the latter by taxes. Consequently, private schools can be more selective, whereas public schools have to accept a percentage of local residents. Don't use "private" or "public" school as a criterion. Instead, decide whether you want to attend a "selective" or "distinguished" school. (You'll get your chance to do this later.)

Note: Many state-supported public university systems, such as the University of California and the State University of New York, have many different campuses but are interrelated when it comes to things like finances, admissions, residency requirements and the like. This can be helpful, for example, if you want to change your major—you may be able to switch schools within the system, rather than having to seek another university entirely. Then again, some public school systems are interrelated in name only. Be sure to find out specifically from the university itself just what options are available within the system.

Colleges vs. Universities?

You'll often hear "college" used as a generic term for any post-high-school institution for advanced learning. In fact, you've read it here numerous times. However, there is a reason why some schools are called colleges and others are called universities. Universities teach both undergraduates and graduates, accommodate many branches of learning and have extensive research facilities. Colleges are usually (but not always) less expansive and more specialized. In any case, the line between the two is fuzzy, so this, too, is probably not a good criterion for choosing.

Liberal-Arts Colleges?

At these schools the goal is not to prepare you for a career so much as to give you a well-rounded, "cultured" education. Liberal-arts administrators also want you to "learn to think critically and analytically." This is why the first two years in a liberal-arts college usually consist of general studies in the arts, humanities and social sciences. You may not have to declare a major until your third year, and, even then, your field may not be career-oriented. If this is the kind of education you want, you may decide in favor of attending a liberal-arts college. However, it's not necessary to attend the typically small, private school to get this kind of education. Universities also encompass liberal-arts colleges.

Learn Anything?

You've just finished reading about a variety of colleges and checking the statements that seemed to apply to you. Did you find that you checked off a number of statements under any one heading? For example, if all four statements under "Denominational Schools" describe your feelings, then you might consider a college affiliated with your religion. Not that you should let the inconclusive statements in this section sway you completely in favor of a denominational school. Again, do a little research first—this book is designed only to give you ideas. In the meantime, indicate below the sorts of schools you think you'll be considering.

☐ Small   ☐ Large   ☐ Size Doesn't Matter
☐ Military
☐ Women's
☐ Black
☐ Liberal Arts
☐ Denominational (Type: _____)
☐ Specialized (Type: _____)
☐ Other

ABSENCE MAKES THE HEART GROW FONDER

Or is it "out of sight, out of mind"? In any case, location is a very big factor in the college search. It's not only a question of how far away from Mom and Dad you should live. You might also wish to move to a different culture or climate. Perhaps you'll want to attend school close to other relatives or friends. Do you thrive in the all-night excitement of a big city or in the flannel-shirt easiness of the country? Or do you not want to change your location at all? That's the first thing you have to decide.

Far Away or Nearby?

Circle True or False.

T F 1. I have to keep my college costs at a bare-bones minimum.

T F 2. I want to stay in close contact with my old friends.

T F 3. I am interested in education— not campus activities.

T F 4. I have reasons for staying at or near home.

T F 5. I can go a long time without coming home.

T F 6. I want the whole traditional college "experience."

T F 7. I want to be on my own as much as possible.

T F 8. I make new friends easily.

Did you answer True to 1–4 and False to 5-8? If this is pretty much how you responded, you should consider attending college in your hometown, perhaps commuting from home.

Did you answer False to 1–4 and True to 5–8? Then you should consider attending a college that is some distance from your home. Go on to the next quiz, *How Far Away?*

Is there no clear indication from your answers whether you're a "townie" or a "traveler"? Check out the pros and cons list on page 52 and then take the next quiz, *How Far Away?* If you're still not sure whether you should stay nearby or go away a distance, don't worry about it. Chances are, you'll be happy either way. So consider local and out-of-town schools—and may the best college win.

WORDS OF WISDOM

"One could argue that Manhattan kids need Maine and that Maine kids need Manhattan during those broadening college years. But academic adjustment and accomplishment through hard work may prove enough of a challenge without also risking a completely foreign locale. To each his own, of course, but teen-agers must seriously examine their ability to adapt to dramatically different surroundings before being won over by the lush brochures put out by both country and city colleges."

—Richard Moll
Playing the Private College Admissions Game

How Far Away?

Circle True or False:

T   F   1. I want to be able to come home on short notice.

T   F   2. I want to stay in-state—it's cheaper.

T   F   3. It's important for me to see current friends on occasion.

T   F   4. I'm not sure I would enjoy a place that is very different from home.

T   F   5. It's okay if I come home only twice a year.

T   F   6. When it comes to tuition and travel costs, money is no object.

T   F   7. I've always wanted to live in a different part of the country.

T   F   8. I'm very independent.

If you answered mostly True to 1–4 and False to 5-8, you're like most college students in that you're probably more suited to live far away from home so you're "away from home," but not so far that you can't jump in a car or bus and get home for the weekend. Consider a school that's within a five-hour drive of where you live.

If you answered mostly False to 1–4 and True to 5–8, you're one of those rare birds who can probably handle a long-distance college. If you've got the money (out-of-state tuition, transportation fares, etc.), you've got lots of options.

If you're not sure, then perhaps finances will be the deciding factor. Don't make the decision yet. Choose colleges at short and long distances. Once you get to the section called *Can You Afford It?*, page 81, the final decision may be determined. Unfortunately, in almost all cases long-distance colleges cost more.

Why I Chose Tri-Cities State Technical Institute
—Blountville, Tennessee

"My school offered me what I was looking for: good technical training. I didn't know much about the field then, but I thought design and drafting were interesting and challenging. When I took mechanical drawing in high school I stayed up all night doing my homework, even though I didn't do that with my other classes. So I looked into Tri-Cities Tech, because I heard it had a good reputation.

"The old 'in-and-out' curriculum also appealed to me. After going to school for twelve years, I didn't know if I wanted to try a four-year curriculum; I wanted something I knew I could complete. I figured I could decide later whether to build on to my associate degree or transfer the credits to something else.

"Tri-Cities Tech was also close by and affordable. I could live at home for free, and the tuition was reasonable for what Tech offered.

"Looking back, I can't complain about my decision. I'm doing better now, financially and otherwise, than I ever expected. The only way I could have gone to a four-year college was if I had had plenty of time and plenty of money. Instead, I got my associate degree in drafting and design in two years, got out and got a job. I think I made the best choice for me."

—Herman Spence
Class of 1983
Mechanical Designer
Atlanta, GA

To Stay or Not to Stay

Need extra help in deciding whether to live at home? Read this list. Add any personal pros and cons.

Living at Home
Pros:

- Cheaper
- Won't miss family and friends
- Already established living arrangements
- Better chance of getting a part-time job
-
-
-

Cons:

- Harder to get involved in campus activities
- Commuting time
- Hard to schedule classes without having empty time during the day
- Fewer opportunities to be independent
-
-
-
-

Living Away from Home
Pros:

- Chance to test a new area
- Learn how to be independent
- Find out more about yourself
-
-
-

Cons:

- More expensive
- Harder to visit home
- Have to do things on your own
-
-
-

Anything Else?

For most people, deciding "how far away" is the biggie. After that, you may or may not be particular about the specifics.

City vs. Country

New York University, located in Manhattan, definitely has a different feel from the University of New Hampshire, located in rural Durham. If you like public transportation, five pizza joints within five minutes and lots of distractions, then the likes of Boston College or Georgetown University may be for you. On the other hand, if you prefer water-skiing to the Smithsonian, foothills to skylines, Hendrix College in Conway, Arkansas, might be more your speed.

Big Town vs. Small

Places like Muncie, Indiana, home of Ball State University, seem to exist for the college alone. There, you're more likely to feel as if you belong, to get around and get what you need. In larger towns or cities, such as Atlanta, where Emory University and Georgia Tech are located, you have to work harder to get your bearings.

Climate and Culture

If the preceding quizzes suggested that you are suited for a long-distance college, you'll also want to consider what climates or cultures might or might not suit you. If you'd like something different from your desert home in Tucson, Arizona, for example, you might consider the forests of Evergreen State College, in Olympia, Washington. On the other hand, if you grew up in a very religious Jewish community in Brooklyn, New York, you might want to bypass the Southern WASP culture at Davidson College, in North Carolina. How do you find out about these things? For first impressions, consult the college guides. *The Fiske Guide to Colleges*, for example, is very candid about the campus environment as well as the makeup of the student body (see also *Student Style,* page 113). Before you actually apply or accept admission to a long-distance school, it's best to visit the campus.

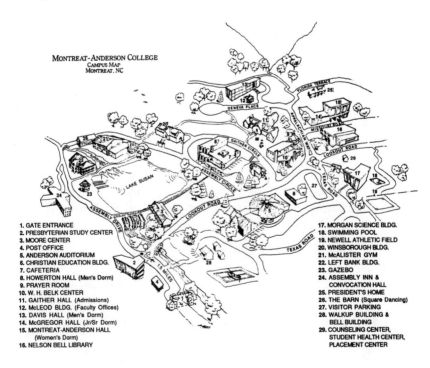

MONTREAT-ANDERSON COLLEGE
CAMPUS MAP
MONTREAT, NC

1. GATE ENTRANCE
2. PRESBYTERIAN STUDY CENTER
3. MOORE CENTER
4. POST OFFICE
5. ANDERSON AUDITORIUM
6. CHRISTIAN EDUCATION BLDG.
7. CAFETERIA
8. HOWERTON HALL (Men's Dorm)
9. PRAYER ROOM
10. W. H. BELK CENTER
11. GAITHER HALL (Admissions)
12. McLEOD BLDG. (Faculty Offices)
13. DAVIS HALL (Men's Dorm)
14. McGREGOR HALL (Jr/Sr Dorm)
15. MONTREAT-ANDERSON HALL
    (Women's Dorm)
16. NELSON BELL LIBRARY

17. MORGAN SCIENCE BLDG.
18. SWIMMING POOL
19. NEWELL ATHLETIC FIELD
20. WINSBOROUGH BLDG.
21. McALISTER GYM
22. LEFT BANK BLDG.
23. GAZEBO
24. ASSEMBLY INN &
    CONVOCATION HALL
25. PRESIDENT'S HOME
26. THE BARN (Square Dancing)
27. VISITOR PARKING
28. WALKUP BUILDING &
    BELL BUILDING
29. COUNSELING CENTER,
    STUDENT HEALTH CENTER,
    PLACEMENT CENTER

54

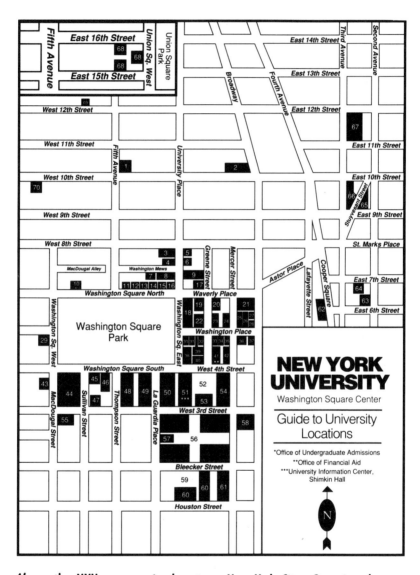

Above, the NYU campus, in downtown New York City. *Opposite,* the more spacious Montreat-Anderson College campus in Montreat, North Carolina. Which would you prefer?

Conclusions

You're a little closer to putting together a pool of schools.

Indicate here your preferred location style. Do you want to go to a college that is:

☐ Far away?　　　☐ Nearby?

If far away, do you want to go to a college that is:

☐ Within five hours' driving distance?

☐ Farther?

What other location specifics do you expect to consider in your college search?

☐ City　　　　　☐ Country　　　☐ Small town
☐ Climate　　　☐ Culture　　　☐ Other

THE OTHER THINGS

Ask someone why he or she chose a particular college. You'll find that a lot of people make their decisions based on the criteria we've already discussed: because it had good programs in a specific field of study, because it was close to home and it was competent in a specific field of study, because it was a small liberal-arts college in a big city...whatever the case may be.

Then there are the people who tell you they chose a school because it resembled someplace else, because a boyfriend or girlfriend attended the college, because relatives did...or "just because."

We call these kinds of reasons "the other things" because they probably aren't the kind of criteria you'll want to depend on. In other words, it's not in your best interests to choose a college simply because it has the best parties in the state.

Even so, we all know that the other things can affect us, that they can make all the difference in the decision. So what the heck—why not play along with the other things for now? If attending the same college that your best friend attends will make you happy, there's no harm in adding that college to your pool of schools. Remember, this section of the book allows you

SOFTWARE TO THE RESCUE!

Tired of leafing through those mammoth college guides, reading the small print and taking reams of notes? Here's good news—the software revolution has made an impressive entrance into the college search process. The College Board and Peterson's, to name just two organizations, have taken the information they publish in books—their databases—and translated it onto floppy disk. What's more, they've added a search facility that can save you an incredible amount of time and effort. Want to know which schools in the state of California offer a major in communications and cost less than $5,000 per year? Just feed in these parameters (there are others, such as size, scholarship availability and required test scores) to build a "personal college profile." Then let the computer handle the job. What might have taken you hours of painstaking (and not very enjoyable) effort can now be done in minutes. High schools across the country have added college-selection and other software to their libraries, guidance offices and career centers. A variety of similar software is available for home use as well. See *References,* page 170, for more information.

to go wild with your choices. In the next section, you'll evaluate the pool of schools and determine whether attending them is realistic. If it happens that the school your best friend attends meets all your criteria, then all the better. Here are some of the prime "other things" to consider:

Social Life

Of course, the college you finally choose should meet your standards for a social life. As you narrow down your pool of schools in Part III—by asking questions, visiting campuses—you'll have a chance to evaluate the scene. But is there a school that (admit it) interests you primarily because of the social prospects? Then let's put it on the list. This is assuming you're already aware of such a college; if not, we don't recommend you go looking for one. But if you must, ask your friends, your older brothers or sisters, college students. Word gets around. Looking for specifics? *Peterson's National College Databank* (see *References,* page 164) offers lists of schools with certain characteristics. You could find out, for example, which colleges have coed dorms, which colleges enroll more than 75 percent men, etc.

Extracurricular Activities
Not exactly the same thing, but close. Let's say you're a powerful tennis player but you plan to major in something unrelated. Still, you're not ready to give up tennis. If a sport— or any other extracurricular activity such as music or theater— is important to you but you don't plan to major in it, consider a school that accommodates your interest anyway. If your sport isn't as common as basketball or football, *Peterson's National College Databank* has a list of schools for twenty-one intercollegiate sports teams. Interested in something else? Ask the high-school teacher who coordinates your activity for suggestions.

Prestige
Plenty of people choose colleges because they're prestigious. What's wrong with that? Nothing, as long as the college is worthy of the label and meets all your needs; this is not always the case. But if the dream of attending Cornell or Stanford makes life worth living, give it a shot.

Tradition/Parents
Perhaps every male member of your family has attended the same university since the dawn of time. That's a tough tradition to break. This is for all the colleges that have to be considered because it's Dad's dream/Dad went there/Dad says you have to go there.

You Name It
There's an "other thing" for everybody. Maybe a school intrigues you because it's got the best football team in the Southeastern Conference, or because Elvis lived near there. This is your chance to indulge those neurotic reasons that rarely come to light.

THE TOP 10 COLLEGE TOWNS*

Which college towns have the best mix of bookishness and ball games? Which are big enough to accommodate a selection of theater and pizza parlors, but small enough to feel like home? According to Edward B. Fiske, education columnist for the *The New York Times*, these are ideal.

Town	College
1. Amherst, Massachusetts	Amherst College
	Hampshire College
	Mount Holyoke College
	Smith College
	University of Massachusetts
2. Austin, Texas	University of Texas at Austin
	Concordia Lutheran College
	Huston-Tillotson College
	St. Edward's University
3. Baton Rouge, Louisiana	Louisiana State University
	Southern University and Agricultural and Mechanical College
4. Bloomington, Indiana	Indiana University
5. Boston/Cambridge, Massachusetts	Harvard University
	Massachusetts Institute of Technology
	Boston College
	Boston University
	Wellesley College
	Simmons College
	Tufts University
	Berklee College of Music
	Boston State College
	Boston Conservatory of Music
	Emerson College
	Emmanuel College
	Hellenic College

Lesley College
University of Massachusetts
Massachusetts College of Art
Massachusetts College of
    Pharmacy and Allied Health
    Sciences
Suffolk University
Wentworth Institute of
    Technology
Bay State Junior College
Chamberlayne Junior College
Fisher Junior College
Franklin Institute of Boston
Laboure College
New England Conservatory of
    Music
St. John's Seminary College
Hebrew College
New England College of
    Optometry

6. Boulder, Colorado	University of Colorado
7. Burlington, Vermont	University of Vermont Champlain College Trinity College Burlington College
8. Chapel Hill, North Carolina	University of North Carolina
9. Eugene, Oregon	University of Oregon Northwest Christian College Eugene Bible College
10. Tempe, Arizona	Arizona State University

*Source: "The Big 10 of College Towns," *The New York Times*, April 6, 1988. (You'll notice that some of the colleges listed are not in the city proper, especially with respect to the Boston/ Cambridge area. This is because the idea of the "college towns" often exceeds any facts represented on maps.)

ASSEMBLING YOUR POOL OF SCHOOLS

Have you decided on a field of study? If so, begin by selecting at least two colleges that excel in your major. They don't have to be the best in the country or miles away, but they should be respected in your field. Ask someone in the field to recommend some colleges— a teacher or someone with a related career. Leaf through college guidebooks. *The Fiske Guide to Colleges*, for example, comments on the quality of various departments in the colleges.

1. _____
2. _____
3. _____
4. _____
5. _____
6. _____
7. _____
8. _____
9. _____
10. _____

What did you learn from the section *From Big Fish to Little Fish?* List some schools that meet the criteria. Large or small college? Specialized?

Location. Did you decide that a college close to home or far away from home is best? It's okay to have a mixture of the two on your prospective list. However, if you've got your heart set on living in your hometown, be sure to list some local colleges.

The Other Things: social life, extracurricular activities, prestige, parents/tradition or any other factors that pique your interest in a college—add those to the list.

Be sure to include some "sure things" in your list as well as "long shots." Sure things are colleges to which you're almost certain to be accepted: community colleges, state-supported colleges, colleges that call themselves "noncompetitive" or "minimally difficult" to enter. Long shots are highly selective colleges. Your chances of gaining admission to a selective school depend on your academic record, of course, so take your particular situation into consideration. College guidebooks offer this sort of information.

Finances. If finances are an important consideration in your search, be sure that some inexpensive schools are represented in your pool. Tax-supported community and in-state colleges are likely to be inexpensive. But that's not to say that all private schools are expensive. Again, college guidebooks provide this information. (Of course, you should list any colleges likely to offer you a scholarship.)

Your pool of schools should include at least five colleges but no more than 10.

PART III

THE FACTS OF LIFE

Now let's take a good, hard look at that pool of schools. Until now, we've made a point of avoiding details that could rain on your parade. It's time now to address those factors; we'll do so with a minimum of discomfort. The overall objective? To apply a series of questions to your pool of schools.

Can You Get In? (page 66) addresses the question of selectivity. With the help of guidebooks and catalogs, you'll determine whether your chances are good or bad.

Can You Afford It? (page 81) looks at college costs and financial aid.

Is the College Academically Sound? (page 102) evaluates the academic strengths among your pool of schools.

And finally, *Can You Visit*

the Campus? (page 110) gives you a chance to see for yourself how such niceties as social life, student style and the campus measure up.

Once you put your pool of schools through this question-and-answer test, *To Which Schools Will You Apply?* (page 124) helps you select the semifinal choices. Then, in Part IV, you'll let the colleges help you make the "final-final" choice. The hard part—the facts of life—will be over.

But First, a Word About College Guides

College guides are an accessible source of information listing test scores, finances, enrollment, addresses, telephone numbers, selectivity ratings, housing, library holdings, social life—the kind of material that's nice to find *all in one place*, especially in the preliminary stages of your search. (As you get down to the wire, you'll rely more on campus visits and your own research.) We've suggested that you consult them before, and we will again.

Keep in mind, however, that college guides are not the definitive word. "The problem," says Ernest L. Boyer, former U.S. Commissioner of Education, current president of the Carnegie Foundation for the Advancement of Teaching and author of *College: The Undergraduate Experience*, "is that each publication uses its own yardstick to measure excellence or decadence." It's up to you to learn about their differences so you can judge the merit of their content.

There are two basic types of college guides. One offers the facts, plain and simple: school size, requirements for admission, financial-aid availability and so on. Examples are *Barron's Profiles of American Colleges, Peterson's Guide to Four-Year Colleges, Comparative Guide to American Colleges, The Fiske Guide to Colleges* and—the most popular among students—the College Board's *The College Handbook*.

The second type of guide provides some objective information and a lot more of the subjective—quotes from students and professors and the authors' own firsthand, on-the-gossipy-side impressions. Examples of this genre include *Insider's Guide to the Colleges*, by the Yale Daily News; *Lisa Birnbach's College Book*, by Lisa Birnbach; and *The Selective Guide to Colleges*, by Edward B. Fiske.

In a class by themselves are the specialized guides, among them: *The Black Student's Guide to Colleges, Guide to Christian Colleges* and *Peterson's After Scholarships, What?* Some of these are straight-and-narrow, some are tell-it-like-it-is, but all evaluate colleges for their own causes.

Not all guides address all colleges, so begin your appraisal by skimming through several. They are generally available in your guidance counselor's office and at your school or local library. If you're not satisfied with the selection you find, try a library in a nearby city. The guides are expensive (almost all cost more than $10), so it's not practical to buy too many of them. However, if you find that you're making too many trips to the library for the same book or two, or the selection is too outdated, you should probably make the investment. See *References*, page 163, for publishing information.

Which college guides do students use the most? Here are the results of a 1984–1985 Carnegie Foundation survey:

Guide	% of Students Who Use
The College Handbook	54
Barron's Profiles of American Colleges	41
Peterson's Guide to Four-Year Colleges	30
The New York Times' Selective Guide to Colleges	22
Lovejoy's College Guide	19
The College Book	17
Comparative Guide to American Colleges	16
The Gourman Report	15

And a Word About College Catalogs

By now you should have written for and received catalogs for some of the schools in your "pool." As we've pointed out, catalogs are expensive to publish and expensive to mail. Therefore, you may have been given a "viewbook" instead of the actual catalog. Viewbooks are easier to read, but they don't provide as much information as a catalog. What's more, viewbooks are produced more or less to "sell" colleges—which means more photographs of smiling students and less hardnosed information about the institution. You may get some of the information you need, but most likely you'll want more. Luckily, libraries try to keep a good stock of college catalogs—either on paper or on microfilm. Ask a librarian to help you locate the materials you want.

At first glance most catalogs look rather complex. Don't be intimidated. Use the Table of Contents and Index; this book will tell you what to look for as you go along. And be sure to see the most recent volumes; requirements and courses change from year to year.

CAN YOU GET IN?

There's a fine line between quitting without a fight and facing reality. Far too many students take one look at test scores and count themselves out of the competition. But things are not so cut-and-dried. SATs or ACTs *are* taken into consideration, but so are your high-school grades, class rank, extracurricular and school activities and the kinds of high-school classes you take. The answers you write on your application are evaluated, as are any required essays, interviews and letters of recommendation. Selective colleges also pick a number of students with a special talent (sports, music), students with alumni relatives, students who are extremely well rounded and students from minority groups.

So, you see, there's more than one way to catch the eye of an admissions officer. You'll never know if you can get into Princeton or Bowdoin until you try.

STAY THE COURSE

Colleges differ when it comes to high-school course requirements. Put simply, the more selective a college is, the more it requires. If you're considering colleges with tough-to-get-in reputations, it's best to enroll in the most advanced math, science and English classes your high school has to offer. Your college major should also influence your selection of high-school electives. For example, future music majors would benefit from courses such as music theory and chorus. If you plan to go into physical education, you'll want to take more than a minimum of P.E. credits. And so on. Just to be on the safe side, look in the catalogs of the schools you're most likely to attend, under the fields of study you're more likely to enter. The requirements will look something like this:

4 years English
3 years Math
  (1 of Geometry, 2 of Algebra)
2 years Science
  (Biology, Chemistry, Physics)
2 years History
2 years Foreign Language

What about facing reality? Well, there is that fine line. If you scored well below 600 on each of your SATs, you've taken a minimum of English, math and science in high school and you're a long way from the top tenth of your class, Harvard probably is not for you. Notice that we've said *probably*. Trouble is, it's not easy to decipher what colleges want from their applicants. Not only does each school have its own preferences, but statistics and economics play a role in the selection process. Some schools reach out to minorities; others don't. In the past, students of a creative nature were favored; these days, they may be passed over for the technical whiz.

Why I Chose The Citadel
—Charleston, South Carolina

"I first learned about The Citadel from a brochure that came in the mail. The picture of the military cadets caught my attention. A few weeks later, I saw Citadel cadets escorting Miss America contestants on television. I was impressed by their prestige. I was also interested in breaking away from my family in Taunton, Massachusetts. I felt tied down in high school, and the 'cool' thing to do was to go a good distance from home. The Citadel had a good reputation and I thought the discipline would help make me more studious.

"Initially, it was hard to adjust to the strict environment and cultural differences. A lot of emphasis was put on academics, and I never realized how people from the South still talk about losing the Civil War. But I eventually graduated second in my class with a bachelor's degree in chemistry and then went on to earn a master's degree in chemical engineering. I don't think I could have done that if I had chosen another college or university. The Citadel gave me discipline structured to achieve academic recognition—and I can always keep my military honors."

—Craig Leite
Class of 1982
Chemical Engineer
Imperial Chemical Industries, Fayetteville, NC

Not everyone has to bother with the selectivity rigmarole. If you favor public schools—especially those in your community or state—your admission is contingent on fewer factors and the chance of your acceptance is higher, perhaps even definite. Some private schools are minimally competitive or noncompetitive.

The worksheets on the next several pages will help you determine how competitive your pool of schools is and whether you should face reality or give it the old one-two. First, write down your accomplishments. For your grade-point average and class rank, consult your guidance counselor. If you can't remember your course work, your school can provide a transcript. (If you haven't yet completed part of your junior year, you may have to leave some spaces blank.)

YOUR ACCOMPLISHMENTS

Your Grade-Point Average (or equivalent)

Your Class Rank or Percentile

Your Test Scores

SAT: Verbal

     Math

ACT Composite:

Achievement Tests

    1.

    2.

    3.

    4.

YOUR COURSE WORK

9th Grade
(record the grade you earned, too)

FIRST SEMESTER	SECOND SEMESTER	SUMMER SCHOOL
1.		
2.		
3.		
4.		
5.		
6.		

10th Grade
(record the grade you earned, too)

FIRST SEMESTER	SECOND SEMESTER	SUMMER SCHOOL
1.		
2.		
3.		
4.		
5.		
6.		
7.		

11th Grade
(record the grade you earned, too)

FIRST SEMESTER	SECOND SEMESTER	SUMMER SCHOOL
1.		
2.		
3.		
4.		
5.		
6.		
7.		

12th Grade
(record the grade you earned, too)

	FIRST SEMESTER	SECOND SEMESTER	SUMMER SCHOOL
1.			
2.			
3.			
4.			
5.			
6.			
7.			

YOUR SCHOOL ACTIVITIES

Activity/Hours per week/No. years participated/Honors or awards
1.
2.
3.
4.
5.
6.
7.
8.

YOUR EXTRACURRICULAR ACTIVITIES

Activity/Hours per week/No. years participated/Honors or awards

1.

2.

3.

4.

5.

6.

7.

8.

OTHER SCHOOL OR EXTRACURRICULAR DISTINCTIONS

1.

2.

3.

4.

5.

6.

7.

8.

Now let's compare your accomplishments with admissions requirements. From where does this information come? It's in the college catalogs and guides. Start with a catalog from one of your colleges.

Look in the Table of Contents or Index under "admissions" for freshmen or undergraduates. Read the appropriate pages.

In some cases, you won't find any specific requirements. For instance, the California Institute of Technology does not say: "We accept students with a 3.5 high-school grade-point average—only." Instead, the Cal Tech catalog says this:

> The freshman class of approximately 215 is selected on the basis of (1) high grades in certain required high school subjects, (2) results of the College Entrance Examination Board tests [SAT] and (3) recommendations and personal qualifications.

What's more, Cal Tech doesn't give you a cut-off point for test scores, but instead lists the required tests and deadlines. This information is important, in case you apply to the college. If you haven't already, jot down dates in your Timetable on page 18. Also take note of any required tests for which you haven't planned.

Now let's go to the guidebooks. Other admissions information, though unofficial, is usually available in these manuals: *Barron's, Lovejoy's, Peterson's, Fiske*—whichever is easiest for you to obtain. It's better to read more than one, since they differ.

The guidebooks have the same basic facts, but they are organized differently. For example, here's how four guides handled Purdue University's SAT requirements:

Lovejoy's—
"Freshman Admissions...2% of the enrolled freshmen scored above 700 on the verbal SAT....16% of the enrolled freshmen scored above 700 on the math SAT."
Barron's—
"Admissions...The SAT scores of those who enrolled were as follows: Verbal—3% above 700...Math—15% above 700."
The Right College—
"Freshman Profile...2% of freshmen who took SAT scored 700 or over on verbal, 15% scored 700 or over on math."
Fiske—
"SAT Ranges V 400–520 M 480–620"
"Note: Indicates scores of half of entering freshmen."

What do these scores mean? If you're in the top 2 percent, you have a leg up on the competition—but the school may not be challenging enough. If you're in the bottom 25 percent, the college may be too challenging, making your chances of being admitted less likely.

Take this into consideration as you read the catalogs and guidebooks for each college in your pool of schools. Then write your answers to the questionnaires below.

Obviously, you can't believe everything you read. Your goal is to look at the facts and make subjective judgments. If a college catalog states that a C+ high-school grade average is required, and you have a C– average, that's definitely one strike against you. But in most cases, you won't find yourself automatically disqualified. As the Mount Holyoke College catalog puts it: "There is no exact formula which can be applied to all applicants."

Follow this example to assess the entrance requirements of your pool of schools.

School State University

Grades No information available

Standing or percentile 70% in the top fifth

Test scores Only 2% scored as high as I did

Curriculum requirements 4 years English, 3 math, 2 science

Activities and distinctions No special requirements

Other Out-of-State students have somewhat higher requirements. Ninety percent are from public high-school backgrounds.

Based on this information, I would say:

☑ I have a good chance of getting in. (Sure Thing)

☐ The chances of my getting in are small or nonexistent. (Long Shot)

☐ The jury is out. (Maybe, Maybe Not)

School

Grades

Standing or percentile

Test scores

Curriculum requirements

Activities and distinctions

Other

Based on this information, I would say:

- ☐ I have a good chance of getting in. (Sure Thing)
- ☐ The chances of my getting in are small or nonexistent. (Long Shot)
- ☐ The jury is out. (Maybe, Maybe Not)

School

Grades

Standing or percentile

Test scores

Curriculum requirements

Activities and distinctions

Other

Based on this information, I would say:

- ☐ I have a good chance of getting in. (Sure Thing)
- ☐ The chances of my getting in are small or nonexistent. (Long Shot)
- ☐ The jury is out. (Maybe, Maybe Not)

School

Grades

Standing or percentile

Test scores

Curriculum requirements

Activities and distinctions

Other

Based on this information, I would say:

☐ I have a good chance of getting in. (Sure Thing)

☐ The chances of my getting in are small or nonexistent. (Long Shot)

☐ The jury is out. (Maybe, Maybe Not)

School

Grades

Standing or percentile

Test scores

Curriculum requirements

Activities and distinctions

Other

Based on this information, I would say:

☐ I have a good chance of getting in. (Sure Thing)

☐ The chances of my getting in are small or nonexistent. (Long Shot)

☐ The jury is out. (Maybe, Maybe Not)

School

Grades

Standing or percentile

Test scores

Curriculum requirements

Activities and distinctions

Other

Based on this information, I would say:

☐ I have a good chance of getting in. (Sure Thing)
☐ The chances of my getting in are small or nonexistent. (Long Shot)
☐ The jury is out. (Maybe, Maybe Not)

School

Grades

Standing or percentile

Test scores

Curriculum requirements

Activities and distinctions

Other

Based on this information, I would say:

☐ I have a good chance of getting in. (Sure Thing)
☐ The chances of my getting in are small or nonexistent. (Long Shot)
☐ The jury is out. (Maybe, Maybe Not)

School

Grades

Standing or percentile

Test scores

Curriculum requirements

Activities and distinctions

Other

Based on this information, I would say:
- ☐ I have a good chance of getting in. (Sure Thing)
- ☐ The chances of my getting in are small or nonexistent. (Long Shot)
- ☐ The jury is out. (Maybe, Maybe Not)

School

Grades

Standing or percentile

Test scores

Curriculum requirements

Activities and distinctions

Other

Based on this information, I would say:
- ☐ I have a good chance of getting in. (Sure Thing)
- ☐ The chances of my getting in are small or nonexistent. (Long Shot)
- ☐ The jury is out. (Maybe, Maybe Not)

School

Grades

Standing or percentile

Test scores

Curriculum requirements

Activities and distinctions

Other

Based on this information, I would say:

☐ I have a good chance of getting in. (Sure Thing)
☐ The chances of my getting in are small or nonexistent. (Long Shot)
☐ The jury is out. (Maybe, Maybe Not)

School

Grades

Standing or percentile

Test scores

Curriculum requirements

Activities and distinctions

Other

Based on this information, I would say:

☐ I have a good chance of getting in. (Sure Thing)
☐ The chances of my getting in are small or nonexistent. (Long Shot)
☐ The jury is out. (Maybe, Maybe Not)

CAN YOU AFFORD IT?

If only you could determine, here and now, whether you could pay for the colleges in your pool of schools. Unfortunately, this is one game that refuses to be simplified. Not only are financial-aid options too numerous to be put into the proverbial nutshell, but economics and politics change the rules every day. What's more, you have little to say about how much you personally can contribute. When you fill out financial-aid forms, you list your family's income and assets. Based on this information, the government and the colleges decide how much money (if any) they will provide you. You're expected to cough up the rest.

This isn't meant to scare you off, but to fire you up. There is more money out there than you might think there is. And you can find it, provided you: (1) have a good academic record; (2) come from a middle- to lower-income family; (3) look hard; and/or (4) don't stop looking until you've exhausted all the options. You and your parents will have to do much of the research and filling-out of forms, but this book can acquaint you with the process. (If you're an heir to some throne or if your parents own the Chicago Bears, this section may not be of interest to you.)

Here's the Situation

• According to the American Enterprise Institute for Public Policy Research, between 1973 and 1985 the average annual cost of a public college education jumped 143 percent. At private institutions the increase was 199 percent.

• According to the College Board, the average annual cost of attending a four-year public institution in 1987–1988 was $5,604. At four-year private schools the average was $10,199.

• Overall consumer prices rise about 2 percent every year, whereas college costs rise about 6 percent.

• On top of everything else, government and private financial aid are down; in 1987 it totaled $20.5 billion. Even after adjusting for inflation, that's 6 percent less than 1980 levels.

81

WHERE TO LOOK FOR PRIVATE SCHOLARSHIPS

- Your parents' jobs
- Town or city clubs
- YMCA
- 4-H Club
- Jaycees
- Girl Scouts
- Foundations
- Labor unions
- Westinghouse
- United Negro College Fund
- Daughters of the American Revolution
- National Society for Professional Engineers
- Religious Organizations
- American Legion
- YWCA
- Kiwanis
- Chamber of Commerce
- Boy Scouts
- National Honor Society
- Ethnic groups
- Elks
- Beauty Pageants
- Associations or organizations connected with your major

The Difference Between a Resident and Nonresident

It's not only cheaper to attend a public institution in your own state, but in some cases the admissions requirements are easier. For example, the University of California at Berkeley raises its grade-point-average minimum for out-of-staters. So all you have to do is rent an apartment in the state that supports your college, right? Sorry, but it's not that simple. Look in your catalogs under "residency status," and you'll see that you have to live in the state for at least twelve months before you qualify. Most catalogs go on to specify exactly what constitutes legal residency. Typical criteria are as follows: Your parents should have established a permanent home (not a vacation house), be registered as voters, pay state income taxes and so on. If your in-state status is questionable—say, for example, you moved in with your grandmother a few months ago—you'll have to supply proof.

Here's What to Do

Plot these dates on your Timetable.

• **By December of your senior year,** you should have financial-aid forms in your hands. Go to your guidance counselor's office and ask which ones are necessary to file for federal and state aid. (The next section explains more about these forms.) If they're not available at the guidance counselor's office, or if you need more information, see *References,* page 172.

• Give these forms to your parents to fill out and mail as soon after **January 1** as possible.

• **As soon as you receive catalogs** from your pool of schools, check the index for "financial aid." Find out which forms are necessary (they may or may not be the same ones required for federal and state aid). If necessary, get the additional forms from the college, your guidance counselor or from the addresses listed in *References,* page 172, and submit them by the **college's deadline.** Need more information? Contact the financial-aid administrator at the college. Get the phone number or address from the catalog or guidebook, or call the admissions office and ask who you should contact.

• Begin looking for private sources of aid **now.** Your guidance counselor will probably have some suggestions. Also, scan the library and bookstores for helpful books and pamphlets (some titles are listed in *References,* page 172). Check the list on page 82 to see if the sources apply to you.

• Begin working to make extra money **now.** Those in the business of disbursing financial aid expect students to contribute roughly $1,000 for the first year of college. In addition, you're supposed to plunk down 35 percent of your own assets and 5 to 7 percent of your parents'. That's money that won't show up in your financial-aid package.

Here's How (Roughly) This Stuff Works

• Financial-aid forms are designed to indicate the amount of money you need to pay for your education. You're likely to use the FAF (Financial Aid Form) or FFS (Family Financial Statement). The FAF and FFS kill several birds with one stone: In most states, they automatically "sign you up" for aid from the federal government, your state government and the college itself. In some situations, however, other forms are required in addition to, or instead of, the FAF or FFS. Consult your counselor, your college catalogs or *References*, page 172, to find out more.

• Four to six weeks after you mail the financial-aid forms, you'll receive a Student Aid Report (SAR). When actually applying to a college, you'll submit copies of the SAR. This provides the schools with information about your financial needs. If you have no brothers or sisters in college and your parents have a relatively high income, your financial needs will

---

Duke University—Durham, North Carolina
Estimated Expenses, Academic Year 1988-1989

Tuition

Returning Students	$10,600 +
Entering Students	$11,950 +

Residential Fee

Single Room	$2,136–$2,803
Double room	$1,606–$2,113

Food

100% board plan	$2,332
75% board plan	$1,952
Books and Supplies	$470
Student Health Fee	$238

+ For the School of Engineering, the tuition for returning students is $11,485; for entering students, $12,570.

It should be realized that additional expenses will be incurred which will depend to a large extent upon the tastes and habits of the individual. The average Duke student, however, can plan on a budget of approximately $17,750 for entering students and $16,400 for returning students for the academic year. These budgets are all-inclusive except for travel costs and major clothing purchases.

---

be considered smaller—and you'll get less money. The more limited your family's assets are, the higher your needs will be— and the more funds you are likely to receive.

• If and when a school accepts your application, it will also provide you with a financial-aid "offer" or "package." The package lists the expenses you'll be expected to cover and the expenses that financial aid will cover. Financial aid may include grants or scholarships, loans and/or work-study (see *Kinds of Aid*, below), depending on your family's income and the college itself. Schools that are very expensive or are eager for your acceptance may offer a larger package than a school that is overcrowded and not as costly.

Lenoir Community College—Lenoir, North Carolina
Estimated Expenses, Academic Year 1988–1989

In accordance with the basic concepts of comprehensive community colleges, all fees are nominal and are held to a minimum. Tuition per quarter is as follows:

In-State

Full-time 12 or more quarter hours	$ 75.00
Part-time (per quarter hour)	$ 6.25

Out-of-State

Full-time 12 or more quarter hours	$702.00
Part-time (per quarter hour)	$ 58.50

ACTIVITY FEE

Students enrolled in day or night classes, with the exception of senior citizens and full-time employees of the College, will pay a student activity fee fall, winter and spring quarters. The fee schedule is as follows:

12 or more quarter hours	$9.00
7–11 quarter hours	$5.00
2–6 quarter hours	$2.00
Vehicle Registration (per quarter)	$ .25

Kinds of Aid

Not all colleges take part in all these programs (the catalog will tell you), but many do. Here are the options:

Grants or scholarships are the best kind of financial aid, since you don't have to pay them back. They include:

Pell Grant: Provided by the federal government. The government also decides how much you get. The Pell Grant is the rule of thumb for all federal financial aid—you have to apply for it first before you apply for any other aid. Fill out the FAF, FFS, Application for Federal Student Aid (AFSA) or the state forms that students in Pennsylvania, California and Illinois use.

Supplemental Educational Opportunity Grants: Provided by the government, but whether you get it is determined by the college. By applying for the Pell, you automatically apply for the SEOG.

Merit Awards: Provided by the college itself solely on the basis of talent or excellence. The college catalog provides information about the school's merit awards and the necessary applications or auditions.

Private Scholarships: Funds available from religious, civic, regional, corporate and academic organizations (see list, page 82). These groups usually rely on their own application forms.

Loans are offered to most students, especially those who do not display severe financial need. Although they're better than no aid at all, four-year loans can mean ten years of payments after graduation. Consequently, the college that offers you the largest grant and the smallest loan is financially more attractive than the heavy-on-the-loans college. Loans come in all shapes and sizes:

Perkins Loans/National Direct Student Loans: The funds come from the federal government, but your college determines whether you may have them. Interest rate: 5 percent.

Guaranteed Student Loans: The funds come from a local bank or credit union, but your state insures the loan. To get a GSL you must first apply for the Pell Grant. After you've been admitted to and accepted by a college, you apply directly to the lender. Check with your guidance counselor or call the phone number provided in *References,* page 173, to find out if any specific forms are required in your state. Interest rate: 7 to 10 percent.

PLUS Loans: Like the GSL, PLUS funds are provided by a private lender insured by the state. Unlike the GSL, however, the borrowers—parents of college students—do not have to show a need. The catch? Interest rates are higher. Interest rate: Changes every year.

Supplement Loans for Students: Same as PLUS, except the borrowers are college students.

Work-Study programs give you the chance to work and earn money to help pay for school. For example, your financial-aid package may provide for a job in the library or admissions office. Some colleges offer co-op programs allowing students to attend classes every other semester. During ''off'' semesters, students work at a job related to their majors, gain valuable experience and earn school money at the same time.

Until Then . . .

Although you should look for private scholarships now, the real work is in filling out the forms—which you and your parents should do as soon as possible after January 1 of your senior year (some money is distributed on a first-come, first-served basis). It's hard to predict how much and what kind of financial aid you'll get. Nevertheless, it wouldn't hurt to have a rough idea of how much you and your family expect to contribute. Use the chart below. You don't have to write down how much your parents owe or have saved—just ask them how much they plan to contribute toward your first year of college.

How Much Can You Contribute?

Parents plan to pay:	$
Your savings:	$
Estimated money you can earn by then:	$
Income from other sources:	$
	$
	$
	$
TOTAL	$

After you fill out this personal financial résumé, you'll need to make a similar reckoning for each of your college choices. We won't bore you with explaining again how to use the catalogs and guidebooks. Just look under "financial aid," "financial information" and/or "tuition and fees." Most catalogs add up tuition, room and board, books and fees to give you a comprehensive yearly cost. The cost comparison between Duke University and Lenoir Community College on pages 84–85 shows you what this means in practice.

Guidebooks place colleges in one of four or five expense ranges. However you gather your information—from the catalogs or guidebooks, or both—make sure you're consistent from college to college. You can't compare five college costs that include room and board, for example, and five school costs that don't include room and board. And don't forget to plot any dates on your Timetable.

Keep this in mind as well: Colleges that guarantee to meet "demonstrated financial need" of accepted students are colleges worth giving extra thought to. Also pay special attention to statistics that show the average amount of financial-aid packages and how many students receive scholarships. The colleges with the highest figures are more likely to be generous to you, too.

Again, use the following example for your own pool of schools.

School The Institute of Technology
Cost First year— $17,750
Average amount of financial-aid package $ 3,000
Students receiving financial aid 50%
Forms FAF or FFS and school's own application
Form deadline 3/1
☐ Pell Grant
☐ SEOG
☐ Perkins Loans
☐ GSL
☑ PLUS
☐ SLS
☐ Work-study
☐ ROTC
☐ New York State Tuition Assistance Program
☐ Roy F. Bell Scholarship (merit award)
☐ Other state loans
Notes 50% of students work on campus.
Bell scholarschip pays first year of
tuition; call college for application
(615-323-8574), due in February.
No guarantee to meet demonstrated
financial need.

Based on this information, how do you feel about attending this school if you are accepted?
☐ I'm sure I could afford it. (Sure Thing)
☑ I'll go only if financial aid pays for most of it. (Long Shot)
☐ It's iffy. (Maybe, Maybe Not)

School

Cost

Average amount of financial-aid package

Students receiving financial aid

Forms

Form deadline

☐ Pell Grant

☐ SEOG

☐ Perkins Loans

☐ GSL

☐ PLUS

☐ SLS

☐ Work-study

☐ ROTC

☐ New York State Tuition Assistance Program

☐ Roy F. Bell Scholarship (merit award)

☐ Other state loans

Notes

Based on this information, how do you feel about attending this school if you are accepted?

☐ I'm sure I could afford it. (Sure Thing)

☐ I'll go only if financial aid pays for most of it. (Long Shot)

☐ It's iffy. (Maybe, Maybe Not)

School

Cost

Average amount of financial-aid package

Students receiving financial aid

Forms

Form deadline

☐ Pell Grant

☐ SEOG

☐ Perkins Loans

☐ GSL

☐ PLUS

☐ SLS

☐ Work-study

☐ ROTC

☐ New York State Tuition Assistance Program

☐ Roy F. Bell Scholarship (merit award)

☐ Other state loans

Notes

Based on this information, how do you feel about attending this school if you are accepted?

☐ I'm sure I could afford it. (Sure Thing)

☐ I'll go only if financial aid pays for most of it. (Long Shot)

☐ It's iffy. (Maybe, Maybe Not)

School

Cost

Average amount of financial-aid package

Students receiving financial aid

Forms

Form deadline

☐ Pell Grant

☐ SEOG

☐ Perkins Loans

☐ GSL

☐ PLUS

☐ SLS

☐ Work-study

☐ ROTC

☐ New York State Tuition Assistance Program

☐ Roy F. Bell Scholarship (merit award)

☐ Other state loans

Notes

Based on this information, how do you feel about attending this school if you are accepted?

☐ I'm sure I could afford it. (Sure Thing)

☐ I'll go only if financial aid pays for most of it. (Long Shot)

☐ It's iffy. (Maybe, Maybe Not)

School

Cost

Average amount of financial-aid package

Students receiving financial aid

Forms

Form deadline

☐ Pell Grant

☐ SEOG

☐ Perkins Loans

☐ GSL

☐ PLUS

☐ SLS

☐ Work-study

☐ ROTC

☐ New York State Tuition Assistance Program

☐ Roy F. Bell Scholarship (merit award)

☐ Other state loans

Notes

Based on this information, how do you feel about attending this school if you are accepted?

☐ I'm sure I could afford it. (Sure Thing)

☐ I'll go only if financial aid pays for most of it. (Long Shot)

☐ It's iffy. (Maybe, Maybe Not)

School

Cost

Average amount of financial-aid package

Students receiving financial aid

Forms

Form deadline

☐ Pell Grant

☐ SEOG

☐ Perkins Loans

☐ GSL

☐ PLUS

☐ SLS

☐ Work-study

☐ ROTC

☐ New York State Tuition Assistance Program

☐ Roy F. Bell Scholarship (merit award)

☐ Other state loans

Notes

Based on this information, how do you feel about attending this school if you are accepted?

☐ I'm sure I could afford it. (Sure Thing)

☐ I'll go only if financial aid pays for most of it. (Long Shot)

☐ It's iffy. (Maybe, Maybe Not)

School

Cost

Average amount of financial-aid package

Students receiving financial aid

Forms

Form deadline

☐ Pell Grant

☐ SEOG

☐ Perkins Loans

☐ GSL

☐ PLUS

☐ SLS

☐ Work-study

☐ ROTC

☐ New York State Tuition Assistance Program

☐ Roy F. Bell Scholarship (merit award)

☐ Other state loans

Notes

Based on this information, how do you feel about attending this school if you are accepted?

☐ I'm sure I could afford it. (Sure Thing)

☐ I'll go only if financial aid pays for most of it. (Long Shot)

☐ It's iffy. (Maybe, Maybe Not)

School

Cost

Average amount of financial-aid package

Students receiving financial aid

Forms

Form deadline

☐ Pell Grant

☐ SEOG

☐ Perkins Loans

☐ GSL

☐ PLUS

☐ SLS

☐ Work-study

☐ ROTC

☐ New York State Tuition Assistance Program

☐ Roy F. Bell Scholarship (merit award)

☐ Other state loans

Notes

Based on this information, how do you feel about attending this school if you are accepted?

☐ I'm sure I could afford it. (Sure Thing)

☐ I'll go only if financial aid pays for most of it. (Long Shot)

☐ It's iffy. (Maybe, Maybe Not)

School

Cost

Average amount of financial-aid package

Students receiving financial aid

Forms

Form deadline

☐ Pell Grant

☐ SEOG

☐ Perkins Loans

☐ GSL

☐ PLUS

☐ SLS

☐ Work-study

☐ ROTC

☐ New York State Tuition Assistance Program

☐ Roy F. Bell Scholarship (merit award)

☐ Other state loans

Notes

Based on this information, how do you feel about attending this school if you are accepted?

☐ I'm sure I could afford it. (Sure Thing)

☐ I'll go only if financial aid pays for most of it. (Long Shot)

☐ It's iffy. (Maybe, Maybe Not)

School

Cost

Average amount of financial-aid package

Students receiving financial aid

Forms

Form deadline

☐ Pell Grant

☐ SEOG

☐ Perkins Loans

☐ GSL

☐ PLUS

☐ SLS

☐ Work-study

☐ ROTC

☐ New York State Tuition Assistance Program

☐ Roy F. Bell Scholarship (merit award)

☐ Other state loans

Notes

Based on this information, how do you feel about attending this school if you are accepted?

☐ I'm sure I could afford it. (Sure Thing)

☐ I'll go only if financial aid pays for most of it. (Long Shot)

☐ It's iffy. (Maybe, Maybe Not)

School

Cost

Average amount of financial-aid package

Students receiving financial aid

Forms

Form deadline

☐ Pell Grant

☐ SEOG

☐ Perkins Loans

☐ GSL

☐ PLUS

☐ SLS

☐ Work-study

☐ ROTC

☐ New York State Tuition Assistance Program

☐ Roy F. Bell Scholarship (merit award)

☐ Other state loans

Notes

Based on this information, how do you feel about attending this school if you are accepted?

☐ I'm sure I could afford it. (Sure Thing)

☐ I'll go only if financial aid pays for most of it. (Long Shot)

☐ It's iffy. (Maybe, Maybe Not)

HOW COLLEGE FRESHMEN PAID FOR COLLEGE

The UCLA Higher Education Research Institute recently asked 200,000 college freshmen how they paid for college. Here's what they said (more than one answer was accepted):

Source	% of Students Who Used These Sources
Parents/family	70
Savings from summer job	48
Part-time work during college	31
Federal guaranteed loans	23
Other savings	22
Pell Grants	20
College scholarship or grant	19
State scholarship or grant	14
College work-study program	10
Supplemental Education Opportunity Grant	5

Does Private Advice Pay?

They go by many names—college counselors, financial-aid planners, independent counselors—and, like your high-school guidance counselor, they want to get you into the college of your choice with the best possible financial-aid package. You see their business cards in shops, their ads in newspapers, their brochures in the mail.

Unlike your high-school counselor, however, private counselors charge a fee—as much as $75 an hour, or $2,000 on a contract basis. Even so, more and more parents and students are turning to private counselors in the hopes of gaining an edge on the college-search competition. After all, an in-school counselor can have as many as 300 to 600 students to advise at a time, in addition to performing other school duties. The conventional wisdom is that parents and students seem to have lost confidence that they're getting the best advice.

Are these paid counselors/advisers worth the money? Well, there are two sides to every story. Here are the pros and cons.

Pro: You're more likely to get personalized attention whenever you need it, in addition to a wider variety of options.

Con: It costs money, and there's no guarantee that you will get into the college of your dreams or receive more financial aid than you ordinarily would.

Pro: With the help of tests, questionnaires and interviews, a private adviser makes choosing the right college something of a science.

Con: Because private counseling is a new business, it's unregulated. That means you can't be sure a private counselor is qualified to give you this advice.

Pro: Private counselors help you every step of the way during your college search. Some go as far as editing or even writing your essay.

Con: This kind of help may be unethical, and, what's more, it has been known to backfire. Admissions officers can pick out a phony, and this can't help your chances.

Pro: Private counselors know the ins and outs of the complicated financial-aid forms. Much like accountants during tax season, they can advise you on how to shift your assets to get the most aid.

Con: Another ethics problem. The people who can afford a private counselor are the least likely to need the financial aid. With only so many pieces of the financial-aid pie to go around, where does this leave those students who have to figure out the forms on their own?

IS THE COLLEGE ACADEMICALLY SOUND?

Most are, but some have weak areas. You can make a general assessment of a college's academic strength by:

Studying the faculty

Start with the index of the catalog. Look up the departments in which you expect to take several classes (journalism, business, anthropology) and read the faculty list. Are there enough members to handle the number of courses in the department (figure that each will teach three courses each semester)? Compare the departments to others. Do any have decidedly larger staffs? Is the bias in your favor, or against it? Make sure the names aren't littered with asterisks (*) and daggers (†); these indicate part-time status. When faculty is short-staffed, courses are either overcrowded or offered sporadically.

In the back of the catalog, look for information about individual instructors. You should be able to answer "yes" to these questions: Do most have Ph.D.'s? Were they educated at reputable colleges—from varied geographical locales? Is there a fair representation of both old and young (you can judge this by their dates of graduation)?

The guidebooks also provide faculty information. Institutions with high percentages of full-time faculty holding Ph.D.'s are most desirable (90 percent is considered the best). Most catalogs and guidebooks give the student-to-teacher ratio, but this isn't as telling as it might be; college officials have been known to manipulate this figure, and classes vary in size for freshmen, anyway.

One thing that's nice to know but isn't always clear from catalogs and guidebooks is whether the instructors have any *special* qualities that make the college more attractive. For example, creative writers might be drawn to a university featuring seminars with well-known authors, or pre-law students may be intrigued by faculty members who have a practice on the side. And so on.

Why I Chose Stanford University
—Stanford, California

"The fact that Stanford had a national reputation made me fairly certain that—if I could get in—I'd get a quality education. At the time, I didn't know what I wanted to do but I thought I could the find a field at Stanford. Not only did it have a strong program in liberal arts, Stanford also had a strong science and engineering program, so it was a very well-balanced school.

"The only negative point was that Stanford was two and a half hours from Napa Valley—I wanted to go farther away from my home. But I planned to live on the West Coast and didn't see any point in attending a school in the East or Midwest.

"I was accepted at Stanford and I graduated with a degree in economics. After seven years in a major corporation and eighteen years in management consulting and executive search, I ended up moving to the East Coast after all. In 1983 I was asked to come to Washington, D.C., as Deputy Director of White House Personnel under President Reagan. For the two years I held that position, I managed the President's selection of cabinet and sub-cabinet members.

"Today, as president of my own executive-search firm, I use economics only in a very broad sense: I work in the corporate world and my interests are concerned with government. The purpose of my education was not to prepare me for a specific career but to teach me how to think. There's too much pressure on young people to choose a career while they're undergraduates in college. First, it's important to get a good education—I don't care what the field is. I recommend taking a broad program, such as liberal arts, that teaches you how to think. Then go out and see the world and then decide on a career course."

—Richard Kinser
Class of 1958
President
Kinser and Associates
New York, NY

Studying the curriculum

As you assess the faculty, check out the courses in the catalogs. Read the descriptions. Do they excite you? Is there a variety of offerings—in number, in approach and in depth? What do you think about the requirements for your major? Can you find courses that satisfy your requirements and your interests? Are there any appealing programs, such as trips to Europe or tutorial studies? Compare the departments you're most interested in to the others. And, of course, compare one catalog to another.

Checking for accreditation and other distinctions

Accreditation indicates that a college or degree program has met minimum standards for its staff, curriculum and facilities. This information is available in catalogs and in most guidebooks. Look under "accreditation" in the catalog index or "academic character" or "honors" in the guidebooks.

Smith College, for example, is accredited by the New England Association of Schools and Colleges. Appalachian State University is accredited by everything from the American Home Economics Association to the American Chemical Society. What's most important is that your college should be accredited for your particular field of study. For example, music majors are wise to consider colleges accredited by the National Association of Schools of Music. Also, membership in various organizations is a plus, if not a must. Examples include the American Association of University Women and the Council of Colleges of Arts and Sciences.

Finally, institutions with chapters of Phi Beta Kappa, Sigma Xi or Tau Beta Pi are most impressive, since these are honor societies for liberal arts, science and engineering students, respectively. Only institutions of academic strength are granted chapters of these organizations.

Evaluating the facilities

Some things have to be evaluated in person (see *Can You Visit the Campus?*, page 110). However, catalogs and guidebooks contain some facts about the libraries that do give indications about their academic excellence (or lack thereof). Libraries with more than 1,000,000 bound volumes and/or more than

1,000,000 titles on microfilm are extremely impressive, although only 125 of the nation's 2,100 baccalaureate-granting colleges lay claim to such a comprehensive library. Compare the libraries among your pool of schools to determine which are superior.

Computers are not an indication of academic excellence. Yet they definitely qualify as a criterion for the college decision. Like the libraries, some computer information is best judged when you visit the campus. In the meantime, read what the guidebooks have to say. Ideally, computers are available for all students, not just those in a related field of study.

Use the preceding guiding principles to research the academic strength of each college in your pool of schools. Then fill in the following questionnaires. Need a second opinion? Ask teachers and other knowledgeable people about the academic quality of your various schools—word gets around. Or check the academic ratings in the guidebooks. *The Fiske Guide to Colleges*, for example, rates institutions on a scale of one to five stars.

Check the box ☒ if the answer is "yes."

School _____

☐ Does the college meet my criteria for a strong faculty?

☐ Is the faculty large enough?

☐ Does the college meet my criteria for interesting and varied course work?

☐ Does it have the appropriate accreditation?

☐ Is it a member of any associations that are important to me?

☐ Is it a member of an honorary society?

☐ Do the facilities satisfy my expectations and needs?

☐ Does it have any other academic strengths that make a significant impression on me?

Based on the information, I would say:

☐ This college's academic qualities are exceptional. (Winner)

☐ This college is academically unacceptable. (Loser)

☐ I'm not sure about this college's academic merit. (No Contest.)

School _____

- ☐ Does the college meet my criteria for a strong faculty?
- ☐ Is the faculty large enough?
- ☐ Does the college meet my criteria for interesting and varied course work?
- ☐ Does it have the appropriate accreditation?
- ☐ Is it a member of any associations that are important to me?
- ☐ Is it a member of an honorary society?
- ☐ Do the facilities satisfy my expectations and needs?
- ☐ Does it have any other academic strengths that make a significant impression on me?

Based on the information, I would say:

- ☐ This college's academic qualities are exceptional. (Winner)
- ☐ This college is academically unacceptable. (Loser)
- ☐ I'm not sure about this college's academic merit. (No Contest.)

School _____

- ☐ Does the college meet my criteria for a strong faculty?
- ☐ Is the faculty large enough?
- ☐ Does the college meet my criteria for interesting and varied course work?
- ☐ Does it have the appropriate accreditation?
- ☐ Is it a member of any associations that are important to me?
- ☐ Is it a member of an honorary society?
- ☐ Do the facilities satisfy my expectations and needs?
- ☐ Does it have any other academic strengths that make a significant impression on me?

Based on the information, I would say:

- ☐ This college's academic qualities are exceptional. (Winner)
- ☐ This college is academically unacceptable. (Loser)
- ☐ I'm not sure about this college's academic merit. (No Contest.)

School _____
- ☐ Does the college meet my criteria for a strong faculty?
- ☐ Is the faculty large enough?
- ☐ Does the college meet my criteria for interesting and varied course work?
- ☐ Does it have the appropriate accreditation?
- ☐ Is it a member of any associations that are important to me?
- ☐ Is it a member of an honorary society?
- ☐ Do the facilities satisfy my expectations and needs?
- ☐ Does it have any other academic strengths that make a significant impression on me?

Based on the information, I would say:
- ☐ This college's academic qualities are exceptional. (Winner)
- ☐ This college is academically unacceptable. (Loser)
- ☐ I'm not sure about this college's academic merit. (No Contest.)

School _____
- ☐ Does the college meet my criteria for a strong faculty?
- ☐ Is the faculty large enough?
- ☐ Does the college meet my criteria for interesting and varied course work?
- ☐ Does it have the appropriate accreditation?
- ☐ Is it a member of any associations that are important to me?
- ☐ Is it a member of an honorary society?
- ☐ Do the facilities satisfy my expectations and needs?
- ☐ Does it have any other academic strengths that make a significant impression on me?

Based on the information, I would say:
- ☐ This college's academic qualities are exceptional. (Winner)
- ☐ This college is academically unacceptable. (Loser)
- ☐ I'm not sure about this college's academic merit. (No Contest.)

School _____

☐ Does the college meet my criteria for a strong faculty?

☐ Is the faculty large enough?

☐ Does the college meet my criteria for interesting and varied course work?

☐ Does it have the appropriate accreditation?

☐ Is it a member of any associations that are important to me?

☐ Is it a member of an honorary society?

☐ Do the facilities satisfy my expectations and needs?

☐ Does it have any other academic strengths that make a significant impression on me?

Based on the information, I would say:

☐ This college's academic qualities are exceptional. (Winner)

☐ This college is academically unacceptable. (Loser)

☐ I'm not sure about this college's academic merit. (No Contest.)

School _____

☐ Does the college meet my criteria for a strong faculty?

☐ Is the faculty large enough?

☐ Does the college meet my criteria for interesting and varied course work?

☐ Does it have the appropriate accreditation?

☐ Is it a member of any associations that are important to me?

☐ Is it a member of an honorary society?

☐ Do the facilities satisfy my expectations and needs?

☐ Does it have any other academic strengths that make a significant impression on me?

Based on the information, I would say:

☐ This college's academic qualities are exceptional. (Winner)

☐ This college is academically unacceptable. (Loser)

☐ I'm not sure about this college's academic merit. (No Contest.)

School _____
- [ ] Does the college meet my criteria for a strong faculty?
- [ ] Is the faculty large enough?
- [ ] Does the college meet my criteria for interesting and varied course work?
- [ ] Does it have the appropriate accreditation?
- [ ] Is it a member of any associations that are important to me?
- [ ] Is it a member of an honorary society?
- [ ] Do the facilities satisfy my expectations and needs?
- [ ] Does it have any other academic strengths that make a significant impression on me?

Based on the information, I would say:
- [ ] This college's academic qualities are exceptional. (Winner)
- [ ] This college is academically unacceptable. (Loser)
- [ ] I'm not sure about this college's academic merit. (No Contest.)

School _____
- [ ] Does the college meet my criteria for a strong faculty?
- [ ] Is the faculty large enough?
- [ ] Does the college meet my criteria for interesting and varied course work?
- [ ] Does it have the appropriate accreditation?
- [ ] Is it a member of any associations that are important to me?
- [ ] Is it a member of an honorary society?
- [ ] Do the facilities satisfy my expectations and needs?
- [ ] Does it have any other academic strengths that make a significant impression on me?

Based on the information, I would say:
- [ ] This college's academic qualities are exceptional. (Winner)
- [ ] This college is academically unacceptable. (Loser)
- [ ] I'm not sure about this college's academic merit. (No Contest.)

School _____

- [ ] Does the college meet my criteria for a strong faculty?
- [ ] Is the faculty large enough?
- [ ] Does the college meet my criteria for interesting and varied course work?
- [ ] Does it have the appropriate accreditation?
- [ ] Is it a member of any associations that are important to me?
- [ ] Is it a member of an honorary society?
- [ ] Do the facilities satisfy my expectations and needs?
- [ ] Does it have any other academic strengths that make a significant impression on me?

Based on the information, I would say:

- [ ] This college's academic qualities are exceptional. (Winner)
- [ ] his college is academically unacceptable. (Loser)
- [ ] I'm not sure about this college's academic merit. (No Contest.)

CAN YOU VISIT THE CAMPUS?

You've gleaned about all you can from books and other secondary sources. As you conclude your college search and narrow your selection, you'll become eager to make some firsthand evaluations. Library holdings, scholarships and selectivity ratings may be great, but you've got to like the place to live with it. On the other hand, you're not likely to choose one college over another because it has better salad bars (at least, we hope not). But things like social life, the student body, the campus and the dorms can make or break the quality of your life away at school. You may be working on the best education in the world, but you might not think so when your dorm room is located beneath a stadium that packs in 100,000 every Saturday.

When to Go

Some advisers believe it's best to visit after you've applied to and been accepted by a college. Supposedly, it's easier to visit two or three colleges to make the Which-will-I-accept? decision than visiting five or six to make the Which-will-I-apply-to? decision.

However, there is a serious problem with this reasoning. Colleges usually send out their acceptance notifications around April 15, and they expect to hear a "yes" or "no" from you around May 1. That gives you only two weeks to work out a trip or two. This is no big deal if you're considering schools within fifty miles. But think of the hardship otherwise!

Of course, until now we've suggested you take every opportunity to visit any college, even ones you're not considering. The more colleges you get to know, the better you'll be able to compare the schools in which you are interested. However, as you get closer to application time—from the spring of your junior year through the winter of your senior year—those trips have to count. You've probably already visited some of the selections in your pool of schools. And, after having completed the evaluations we've just been through, you may have mentally eliminated a few schools. Those you don't have to worry about. But it's to your advantage to visit soon the schools you're serious about.

The ideal time to go is Monday through Thursday, when classes are in full swing. The worst times are weekends, holidays, between semesters, exam times or reading periods—any time when students aren't in class and faculty aren't on campus. The idea is to talk to the students and faculty and get a feel for what the college is really like. (Granted, Saturday nights on campus are more colorful than Monday mornings, but...)

Do the best you can with the time you have available. A high-school holiday such as spring vacation may be a good time for you. Perhaps your family vacation itinerary could include some campus visits. Or, if you're a big college-football fan, take in a game on a weekend.

But before you pack a knapsack and hitch a ride to Vegas, call or write the admissions offices of the colleges you'll visit (look in the catalogs or guidebooks for the phone numbers or addresses). They'll be prepared to set a date, give you a tour and inundate you with information. Don't hesitate to ask for catalogs, applications or financial-aid forms you don't have. In some cases, this is also the appropriate time to set up an interview with the admissions staff (see *Interviews: A Thing of the Past?*, page 115). Finally, it makes good sense to check with the admissions office just to be sure your itinerary is in accordance with theirs; you don't want to show up when the school closes down for Groundhog Day or some other obscure yet hallowed university tradition.

Things You Should Do During Your Visits

- Stop by the admissions office.
- Spend a night in a dormitory. (If you don't know any students, ask the admissions office to help you arrange this.)
- Take a tour of the campus.
- Take an "unofficial" walk around campus.
- Eat a meal at a campus cafeteria.
- Talk to any faculty members of special interest—for example, a coach if you're an athlete, or an instructor in your field of study.
- Talk to students in your field of study, in the dormitory, at the library—whenever and wherever you can.
- Get someone to take you on a "tour" of your kind of social life, whether it's nightclubs, ball games, concerts or hiking.
- Visit the library.
- Attend some classes.
- Read the bulletin boards, student newspaper and any other campus publications.
- Interview (optional).

What to Look for

As you check out the library and hobnob with the students, keep an open mind. Try not to let first impressions be your last. Rather, let your image of the institution evolve. Think of yourself as a movie critic. You have to wait until the end before you can really make an evaluation. Then you can look at the good and bad and decide if any of your earlier impressions is true. Following are the kinds of things you should take into consideration.

Social Life

Do social events seem to revolve around fraternities and sororities? Does the nightlife feature alcohol and little else? Do activities fall mostly on the formal or informal side? Are people obsessed with GPA's or the PGA?

The "right" or "wrong" answers depend on your preferences. If you plan to stay on campus until Christmas, then you might have a problem with a college that goes numb on the weekends. If religion isn't an important part of your life, a campus that puts emphasis on church-related events won't suit you. Scan the college newspaper and bulletin boards. Listen to the talk among students in the dormitories and cafeterias. Ask people what they do when they go out.

Student Style

Can you imagine yourself living and studying with these students for a year? Four years? Are they preoccupied with the libraries or the bars? Do they come from well-to-do families, needy families or do they vary? Are they friendly or rude?

Take a good look at yourself before you evaluate the student style that fits you best. Some students feel more comfortable among people who are similar to themselves. Others get restless living in homogeneous societies. Truth is, you'll understand more about your personal values once you go away to college. Until now, you've most likely been living with people like yourself; in college you'll be thrown together with other types. This is good for you! So, for now, try to imagine how you would fit in on a campus that seems somewhat strange or alien to you. Study the students in class, in the dormitories, when they're relaxing at a ball game or in the TV room. Try to get a complete picture of the student style—students of a similar type have been known to flock to one dorm, so you can't assume that your overnight hosts are typical. Look around, and then ask the students themselves about different groups on campus.

Faculty Style

How do they act in class? Bored? Interested? Interesting? Did the students in the class participate, or were they catatonic? What about the instructors you met? Did they ask you about yourself? Could you "connect," or were the instructors difficult to understand?

Obviously, you can't make sweeping generalizations after meeting with the instructor of introductory philosophy for five minutes. But you should feel good about the faculty in your field of study. Ask students what they think of the instructors:

Do they avail themselves to students, or is it virtually impossible to get an appointment? Does teaching seem to take a backseat with the faculty—are they more interested in research or writing? Don't hesitate to ask questions of the faculty members as well: What is the quality of the student-faculty relationships? How many students are in your classes?

Facilities

On page 104, you were told to assess the quality of the libraries by reading the catalogs and guidebooks. Here's your chance to do it in person. First, pay attention to where the students do their studying. Are the dorms quiet enough? Or do students head to the library for solitude? If that's the case, make sure the library itself is quiet. Is it open late? On the weekends? If you anticipate doing a lot of work at the library, it won't do you much good if it shuts down at 6:00 on Friday night. Check the seating availability. Is it jam packed on the weeknights? Are there cubicles and obscure little corners where you can concentrate? Ask the students these questions as well. There may be problems—or solutions—not immediately evident.

And, of course, you'll want to judge the cafeterias, the dormitories, the athletic facilities, the bookstores, the classroom buildings, the student center, the infirmary. A word to the wise: Don't expect the dormitories to be new and spacious. The food probably won't knock your socks off, either. This is college, after all, and you're not supposed to be living in the lap of luxury. Nevertheless, it's not too much to ask that your dormitory be comfortable and your food be edible. Decide what you must have and what you can live with. Ask the students about their gripes as well.

The Campus

In Part II you made decisions about the ideal campus. So, what do you think? Is the prospect of living in the big city so thrilling that you can't get the "little-town-blues-are-melting-away" verse out of your head? Or did your first ride in a taxicab send you reeling? What did it feel like when you were walking around on campus—did the rolling hills stir you to a perpetual state of bliss? Or did those rolling hills leave you with nothing but blisters and perspiration stains? Is there adequate shopping, transportation and police protection to suit you? You'd be surprised how much your gut reactions will tell you about a campus.

Interviews: A Thing of the Past?

Most colleges still grant interviews, but fewer and fewer require them. Not only do schools receive more applications than they can accommodate, but according to a 1989 *New York Times* article, admissions officers say that interviews aren't necessary. Because so many items are evaluated—essays, letters of recommendation, transcripts, extracurricular activities—the interview rarely reveals anything surprising about a candidate. What's more, admissions staffs don't think it's fair to count personal appearances on campuses for the people who arrange them because there are so many people who don't or can't.

Still, most counselors believe that interviews are a good idea for most students, particularly if you need to explain bad grades or a lack of college-preparatory course work. Students who have dynamic personalities or who might improve the impressions they make on paper would also be wise to consider an interview.

Check with the admissions offices to see if interviews are recommended or required—and when. Find out who your interviewer will be. Most likely, it will be an admissions counselor on campus, but some schools have students or alumni come to your hometown to do the honors.

In any case, research the catalogs and guidebook information about the college before you arrive. Dress neatly. Be on time. Bring your transcript and a résumé. Listen to the interviewer; don't interrupt and be sure you understand her questions. Try not to be nervous, but if you are, don't get angry at yourself and make the situation worse. Almost everybody gets nervous on interviews—you will when you apply for a job someday, too. Anyway, it's nice to know you're getting practice for something you'll have to do again and again. It helps to rehearse your answers to the questions. Also, don't forget to have your own questions on hand—you're expected to.

The Fine Art of Asking Questions

It's tricky for us to give you questions to ask. Your questions should come from you. Ask about things you genuinely want to know.

From the very beginning of your college search, be free with your questions. Talk to people who work in fields of studies that interest you. Talk to alumni, college students, other high-school students, teachers and campus representatives. Don't be shy, particularly when you visit the colleges. You'll find that college students enjoy telling you what they think; it makes them feel important when you request their help. The same goes for faculty and admissions officers; they're obliged to tell you what you want to know.

There is a smart way of going about the "inquisition," however. Be polite and appreciative, not pushy and critical. Be confident but not conceited. Don't just blurt out any question that comes to mind; questions that are too general (Can you tell me about all 48 departments?) or that can be found in the catalog (What does it cost to attend?) are uncalled for. Instead, think through and write down your questions ahead of time. You will also benefit from jotting down your impressions in a notebook at the end of an interview or visit. Of course, you don't have to be as formal with college students as you will be with college officials. Even so, you'll go a lot further with everyone by showing them your respect. And always, always thank people for taking the time to talk to you. Follow up with a thank-you letter and you get a gold star.

What If You Can't Visit?

If you're serious about a college, you really should try to arrange a visit. Attending a college without having seen it is risky business. But this is the real world, and most of us aren't so well off that we can trot off to New York or California on a whim. What does one do then?

The most obvious option is to see first if a far-reaching college accepts you. If it does, then do your darnedest to get out there before you accept. If that's still out of the question, you're between a rock and a hard spot. Try contacting the admissions office that accepted you to see if it has any suggestions (this may not turn up anything but it's worth a shot). Otherwise, before you apply to or accept a college you cannot visit, make sure you do the following:

• Go back to the guidebooks and catalogs. Depending on the type of guidebooks you read, you can get different kinds of information on social life, facilities, student style, the campus and so on (see *But First, a Word About College Guides,* page 64). Catalogs provide real-life information along the "official" side (meaning boring and hard to see through). Nevertheless, you should study the pictures, the campus map and any other information that is provided.

• Ask your guidance counselor for names of students who graduated from your high school and who now attend the college. Or write to the admissions office for names of students or recent alumni who live in your area. Contact some of these people and ask all your questions.

• Attend all college fairs that come to town at which yours will be represented. The admissions office can tell you about these.

• Have the admissions office arrange for interviews in your hometown.

• Ask the admissions office if there are any videos of the campus. In fact, you may have run across campus videos before—through advertising, the library or your high school. Seeing a video is certainly better than not seeing the campus at all, but it's not close enough. Keep in mind that these videos are often developed by people who want to make the college look good. That means you will see the brand-spanking-new sports arena, but you won't see the jazz band rehearsing in a garage.

Here's another form that will help you put all of the preceding suggestions into action.

School **Smith and Jones University**

Social Life
☐Agrees with Me ☑Doesn't Agree with Me ☐Is Just Okay

Student Style
☑Agrees with Me ☐Doesn't Agree with Me ☐Is Just Okay

Faculty Style
☐Agrees with Me ☑Doesn't Agree with Me ☐Is Just Okay

Facilities
☐Agree with Me ☐Don't Agree with Me ☑Are Just Okay

The Campus
☑Agrees with Me ☐Doesn't Agree with Me ☐Is Just Okay

Notes **More impressed with the student aquatic center than other facilities. I personally wasn't impressed with the faculty, but other students say good things.**

School
Social Life
☐Agrees with Me ☐Doesn't Agree with Me ☐Is Just Okay

Student Style
☐Agrees with Me ☐Doesn't Agree with Me ☐Is Just Okay

Faculty Style
☐Agrees with Me ☐Doesn't Agree with Me ☐Is Just Okay

Facilities
☐Agree with Me ☐Don't Agree with Me ☐Are Just Okay

The Campus
☐Agrees with Me ☐Doesn't Agree with Me ☐Is Just Okay

Notes

School
Social Life
☐Agrees with Me ☐Doesn't Agree with Me ☐Is Just Okay

Student Style
☐Agrees with Me ☐Doesn't Agree with Me ☐Is Just Okay

Faculty Style
☐Agrees with Me ☐Doesn't Agree with Me ☐Is Just Okay

Facilities
☐Agree with Me ☐Don't Agree with Me ☐Are Just Okay

The Campus
☐Agrees with Me ☐Doesn't Agree with Me ☐Is Just Okay

Notes

School
Social Life
☐Agrees with Me ☐Doesn't Agree with Me ☐Is Just Okay

Student Style
☐Agrees with Me ☐Doesn't Agree with Me ☐Is Just Okay

Faculty Style
☐Agrees with Me ☐Doesn't Agree with Me ☐Is Just Okay

Facilities
☐Agree with Me ☐Don't Agree with Me ☐Are Just Okay

The Campus
☐Agrees with Me ☐Doesn't Agree with Me ☐Is Just Okay

Notes

School
Social Life
☐Agrees with Me ☐Doesn't Agree with Me ☐Is Just Okay

Student Style
☐Agrees with Me ☐Doesn't Agree with Me ☐Is Just Okay

Faculty Style
☐Agrees with Me ☐Doesn't Agree with Me ☐Is Just Okay

Facilities
☐Agree with Me ☐Don't Agree with Me ☐Are Just Okay

The Campus
☐Agrees with Me ☐Doesn't Agree with Me ☐Is Just Okay

Notes

School
Social Life
☐Agrees with Me ☐Doesn't Agree with Me ☐Is Just Okay

Student Style
☐Agrees with Me ☐Doesn't Agree with Me ☐Is Just Okay

Faculty Style
☐Agrees with Me ☐Doesn't Agree with Me ☐Is Just Okay

Facilities
☐Agree with Me ☐Don't Agree with Me ☐Are Just Okay

The Campus
☐Agrees with Me ☐Doesn't Agree with Me ☐Is Just Okay

Notes

School
Social Life
☐Agrees with Me ☐Doesn't Agree with Me ☐Is Just Okay

Student Style
☐Agrees with Me ☐Doesn't Agree with Me ☐Is Just Okay

Faculty Style
☐Agrees with Me ☐Doesn't Agree with Me ☐Is Just Okay

Facilities
☐Agree with Me ☐Don't Agree with Me ☐Are Just Okay

The Campus
☐Agrees with Me ☐Doesn't Agree with Me ☐Is Just Okay

Notes

School
Social Life
☐Agrees with Me ☐Doesn't Agree with Me ☐Is Just Okay

Student Style
☐Agrees with Me ☐Doesn't Agree with Me ☐Is Just Okay

Faculty Style
☐Agrees with Me ☐Doesn't Agree with Me ☐Is Just Okay

Facilities
☐Agree with Me ☐Don't Agree with Me ☐Are Just Okay

The Campus
☐Agrees with Me ☐Doesn't Agree with Me ☐Is Just Okay

Notes

School
Social Life
☐Agrees with Me ☐Doesn't Agree with Me ☐Is Just Okay

Student Style
☐Agrees with Me ☐Doesn't Agree with Me ☐Is Just Okay

Faculty Style
☐Agrees with Me ☐Doesn't Agree with Me ☐Is Just Okay

Facilities
☐Agree with Me ☐Don't Agree with Me ☐Are Just Okay

The Campus
☐Agrees with Me ☐Doesn't Agree with Me ☐Is Just Okay

Notes

School
Social Life
☐Agrees with Me ☐Doesn't Agree with Me ☐Is Just Okay

Student Style
☐Agrees with Me ☐Doesn't Agree with Me ☐Is Just Okay

Faculty Style
☐Agrees with Me ☐Doesn't Agree with Me ☐Is Just Okay

Facilities
☐Agree with Me ☐Don't Agree with Me ☐Are Just Okay

The Campus
☐Agrees with Me ☐Doesn't Agree with Me ☐Is Just Okay

Notes

School

Social Life

☐Agrees with Me ☐Doesn't Agree with Me ☐Is Just Okay

Student Style

☐Agrees with Me ☐Doesn't Agree with Me ☐Is Just Okay

Faculty Style

☐Agrees with Me ☐Doesn't Agree with Me ☐Is Just Okay

Facilities

☐Agree with Me ☐Don't Agree with Me ☐Are Just Okay

The Campus

☐Agrees with Me ☐Doesn't Agree with Me ☐Is Just Okay

Notes

TO WHICH SCHOOLS WILL YOU APPLY?

Now let's compile your evaluations for each college into one super chart that tells it all. The questions and boxes below will look familiar. Turn back to the pages that contain your answers for each question and rewrite them here.

School
Can I get in?
☐ Sure Thing   ☐ Long Shot   ☐ Maybe, Maybe Not

Can I afford it?
☐ Sure Thing   ☐ Long Shot   ☐ Maybe, Maybe Not

Is the college academically sound?
☐ Winner   ☐ Loser   ☐ No Contest

Can I visit the campus?
Social Life   ☐ Agrees   ☐ Doesn't Agree   ☐ Just Okay
Student Style   ☐ Agrees   ☐ Doesn't Agree   ☐ Just Okay
Faculty Style   ☐ Agrees   ☐ Doesn't Agree   ☐ Just Okay
Facilities   ☐ Agrees   ☐ Doesn't Agree   ☐ Just Okay
Campus   ☐ Agrees   ☐ Doesn't Agree   ☐ Just Okay

School
Can I get in?
☐Sure Thing   ☐Long Shot   ☐Maybe, Maybe Not

Can I afford it?
☐Sure Thing   ☐Long Shot   ☐Maybe, Maybe Not

Is the college academically sound?
☐Winner   ☐Loser   ☐No Contest

Can I visit the campus?
Social Life	☐Agrees	☐Doesn't Agree	☐Just Okay
Student Style	☐Agrees	☐Doesn't Agree	☐Just Okay
Faculty Style	☐Agrees	☐Doesn't Agree	☐Just Okay
Facilities	☐Agrees	☐Doesn't Agree	☐Just Okay
Campus	☐Agrees	☐Doesn't Agree	☐Just Okay

School

Can I get in?
☐Sure Thing   ☐Long Shot   ☐Maybe, Maybe Not

Can I afford it?
☐Sure Thing   ☐Long Shot   ☐Maybe, Maybe Not

Is the college academically sound?
☐Winner   ☐Loser   ☐No Contest

Can I visit the campus?
Social Life	☐Agrees	☐Doesn't Agree	☐Just Okay
Student Style	☐Agrees	☐Doesn't Agree	☐Just Okay
Faculty Style	☐Agrees	☐Doesn't Agree	☐Just Okay
Facilities	☐Agrees	☐Doesn't Agree	☐Just Okay
Campus	☐Agrees	☐Doesn't Agree	☐Just Okay

School

Can I get in?
☐Sure Thing   ☐Long Shot   ☐Maybe, Maybe Not

Can I afford it?
☐Sure Thing   ☐Long Shot   ☐Maybe, Maybe Not

Is the college academically sound?
☐Winner   ☐Loser   ☐No Contest

Can I visit the campus?
Social Life   ☐Agrees   ☐Doesn't Agree   ☐Just Okay
Student Style   ☐Agrees   ☐Doesn't Agree   ☐Just Okay
Faculty Style   ☐Agrees   ☐Doesn't Agree   ☐Just Okay
Facilities   ☐Agrees   ☐Doesn't Agree   ☐Just Okay
Campus   ☐Agrees   ☐Doesn't Agree   ☐Just Okay

School

Can I get in?
☐Sure Thing   ☐Long Shot   ☐Maybe, Maybe Not

Can I afford it?
☐Sure Thing   ☐Long Shot   ☐Maybe, Maybe Not

Is the college academically sound?
☐Winner   ☐Loser   ☐No Contest

Can I visit the campus?
Social Life   ☐Agrees   ☐Doesn't Agree   ☐Just Okay
Student Style   ☐Agrees   ☐Doesn't Agree   ☐Just Okay
Faculty Style   ☐Agrees   ☐Doesn't Agree   ☐Just Okay
Facilities   ☐Agrees   ☐Doesn't Agree   ☐Just Okay
Campus   ☐Agrees   ☐Doesn't Agree   ☐Just Okay

School

Can I get in?
☐Sure Thing   ☐Long Shot   ☐Maybe, Maybe Not

Can I afford it?
☐Sure Thing   ☐Long Shot   ☐Maybe, Maybe Not

Is the college academically sound?
☐Winner   ☐Loser   ☐No Contest

Can I visit the campus?
Social Life   ☐Agrees   ☐Doesn't Agree   ☐Just Okay
Student Style ☐Agrees   ☐Doesn't Agree   ☐Just Okay
Faculty Style ☐Agrees   ☐Doesn't Agree   ☐Just Okay
Facilities   ☐Agrees   ☐Doesn't Agree   ☐Just Okay
Campus   ☐Agrees   ☐Doesn't Agree   ☐Just Okay

School

Can I get in?
☐Sure Thing   ☐Long Shot   ☐Maybe, Maybe Not

Can I afford it?
☐Sure Thing   ☐Long Shot   ☐Maybe, Maybe Not

Is the college academically sound?
☐Winner   ☐Loser   ☐No Contest

Can I visit the campus?
Social Life   ☐Agrees   ☐Doesn't Agree   ☐Just Okay
Student Style ☐Agrees   ☐Doesn't Agree   ☐Just Okay
Faculty Style ☐Agrees   ☐Doesn't Agree   ☐Just Okay
Facilities   ☐Agrees   ☐Doesn't Agree   ☐Just Okay
Campus   ☐Agrees   ☐Doesn't Agree   ☐Just Okay

School

Can I get in?
☐Sure Thing   ☐Long Shot   ☐Maybe, Maybe Not

Can I afford it?
☐Sure Thing   ☐Long Shot   ☐Maybe, Maybe Not

Is the college academically sound?
☐Winner   ☐Loser   ☐No Contest

Can I visit the campus?

Social Life	☐Agrees	☐Doesn't Agree	☐Just Okay
Student Style	☐Agrees	☐Doesn't Agree	☐Just Okay
Faculty Style	☐Agrees	☐Doesn't Agree	☐Just Okay
Facilities	☐Agrees	☐Doesn't Agree	☐Just Okay
Campus	☐Agrees	☐Doesn't Agree	☐Just Okay

School

Can I get in?
☐Sure Thing   ☐Long Shot   ☐Maybe, Maybe Not

Can I afford it?
☐Sure Thing   ☐Long Shot   ☐Maybe, Maybe Not

Is the college academically sound?
☐Winner   ☐Loser   ☐No Contest

Can I visit the campus?

Social Life	☐Agrees	☐Doesn't Agree	☐Just Okay
Student Style	☐Agrees	☐Doesn't Agree	☐Just Okay
Faculty Style	☐Agrees	☐Doesn't Agree	☐Just Okay
Facilities	☐Agrees	☐Doesn't Agree	☐Just Okay
Campus	☐Agrees	☐Doesn't Agree	☐Just Okay

School

Can I get in?
☐Sure Thing   ☐Long Shot   ☐Maybe, Maybe Not

Can I afford it?
☐Sure Thing   ☐Long Shot   ☐Maybe, Maybe Not

Is the college academically sound?
☐Winner   ☐Loser   ☐No Contest

Can I visit the campus?
Social Life	☐Agrees	☐Doesn't Agree	☐Just Okay
Student Style	☐Agrees	☐Doesn't Agree	☐Just Okay
Faculty Style	☐Agrees	☐Doesn't Agree	☐Just Okay
Facilities	☐Agrees	☐Doesn't Agree	☐Just Okay
Campus	☐Agrees	☐Doesn't Agree	☐Just Okay

Finally, Choose the Schools to Which You'll Apply

A. Notice that the first column of boxes under each school records positive answers. A school that shapes up something like this is a school you obviously favor:

☒ Sure Thing
☒ Sure Thing
☒ Winner
☒ Agrees
☒ Agrees
☒ Agrees
☒ Agrees
☒ Agrees

B. Notice that the second column of boxes under each school records negative answers. A school that shapes up something like this is a school about which you have doubts:

☒ Long Shot
☒ Long Shot

☒ Loser

☒ Doesn't Agree

☒ Doesn't Agree

☒ Doesn't Agree

☒ Doesn't Agree

☒ Doesn't Agree

C. The third column is for middle-of-the-road answers. They'll have little influence on your decision.

D. By now you should be ready to pick your favorite colleges. Put a "1" after your first choice, like this:

School: University of Missouri at Columbia   <u> 1 </u>

Your first choice won't necessarily be the college with the most marked boxes in column one, although it ought to have a few. Instead, your first choice should be the college that you feel best about, in view of all the research you've done.

E. Continue to rate the colleges in your order of preference, from 1 to 10.

F. To which schools will you apply? At least two, but no more than five. Go ahead and write down your first choice after 1, regardless of whether it's a Long Shot or a Sure Thing.

G. You'll want at least one other choice. If 1 is a Long Shot (as described in the sections titled *Can You Get In?* or *Can You Afford It?*, pages 66 and 81, respectively), be sure 2 is a Sure Thing. If you plan to apply to only two colleges, 2 has to be a Sure Thing in terms of both *Can You Get In?* and *Can You Afford It?* If 1 is a Sure Thing, 2 can be your second-favorite school.

H. If you plan to apply to more than two colleges, write down more of your favorite college choices. Be sure to balance the Long Shots with the Sure Things. You always want Sure Thing colleges to fall back on—colleges you are sure you'll be accepted to and/or colleges you are sure you can afford. Then you'll feel more confident about taking a risk and applying to one or two Long Shots.

Write in the schools you'll apply to:

1. _____   4. _____

2. _____   5. _____

3. _____

P A R T   I V

CAMPUS BOUND!

That wasn't so bad, was it? Just a few more steps, and then you can enjoy the final months of your senior year, and the summer ahead, secure with the knowledge that you've got a great year in a great school awaiting you.

First, there is the application process. The section called *Ready, Set, Go* gives you easy suggestions for organizing and completing the paper work. Don't forget to seek out the expert advice of your counselor and your parents. Make sure you complete the personal part of the application.

When the Verdicts Come In helps you evaluate the replies you get from your colleges. How do you handle rejection? Wait lists? What criteria should you use when you're making the final-final decision?

And finally, *So You Won't Be Surprised* offers parting-shot information for the transition from high-school senior to college freshman. Birds gotta fly, fish gotta swim.

READY, SET, GO

Guidance counselors and admissions officers often complain that high-school students don't take the necessary pains with their applications. The long answers aren't thoroughly developed, they say, or the short answers are underestimated. And they're right, for the most part. Filling out an application involves more than just submitting it on time. Here are some pointers:

• Make note of the application deadlines on your Timetable. Work on the applications in order of their deadlines. Allow as much time as possible per application—a day or two isn't enough. You'll want to think about the questions, write outlines, do rough drafts and revise them a few times.

• Make photocopies of each application. Write your answers on the photocopies before you write on the original form.

• Read directions carefully. If a handwritten application is required, then by all means write it yourself. If typing is permissible, type if you are able to, but don't let anyone else do the honors. Your own neat handwriting is preferable to your mom's secretary's neat typing.

• Select carefully the activities and awards you list. Choose quality over quantity. It's better to fill the space with five or six impressive, long-term achievements, for example, than to cram in everything from baton-twirling lessons to a couple of weeks on the yearbook staff.

• Look for discrepancies; strive for consistency. There are only 168 hours in a week, so it's not possible for you to run track 40 hours, study 40 hours, do volunteer work 40 hours and still have time to sleep and go to school. At the same time, you don't want to wax eloquent on your dream to be an artist on one page, only to mark accounting as your field of interest on the next page.

• Write in your own words. Admissions officers don't want

Thomas Wolfe, they want you. If you're using words that don't come naturally to you, it will show. Obey every grammar rule and strive for lively, interesting prose, but keep it simple.

• Don't pass up an opportunity to write an essay when it's suggested but not required. Take extreme pride in this part of your application—it can make a tremendous impression. Make sure your essays show character, depth of feeling, self-discipline, an interest in education, your goals and any other admirable qualities.

• Approach an essay so that it interests you. This is the secret to enjoyable writing. For example, explain how your favorite movie addresses your personal goals. Or describe a childhood incident and how it set you on the path to becoming a doctor.

• Write separate essays for each college.

• Don't be afraid to state your strengths. This is no time for modesty. At the same time, don't hedge any shortcomings. That's not to say you should put yourself down, but there's nothing wrong with admitting that writing isn't your forte or that you're not as aggressive as you'd like to be. Do end on an upbeat note, however, by saying that you're improving in this area or you hope the college can help you overcome the problem.

• Pay attention to details. Don't leave any spaces blank. Double-check spellings, addresses, code numbers and due dates. Be sure to include any required fees as well as required financial-aid forms, transcripts, test scores or letters. (In many cases, you won't send this information with your application, but you will ask your school or other parties to submit it.)

About Those Essays . . .

What kinds of essays will you be expected to write? Here are some sample questions:

• "What are your academic goals?" (Syracuse University—Syracuse, New York)

• "Write an autobiographical statement." (University of California, Berkeley—Berkeley, California)

• "What's the most important activity in which you are involved?" (Yale University—New Haven, Connecticut)

Why I Chose to Study Abroad: Hebrew University
—Jerusalem, Israel

"A year of study abroad is like having an entire country for a university, and nowhere is this more true than in Jerusalem, that ancient crossroads of cultures and civilizations. Ten years ago, having completed my degree requirements and seeking to further my knowledge, I decided to continue my studies of religion in that sacred center of the three great Western religions.

"I recall one evening, sitting in my room in the Jewish quarter, located inside the ancient walls of the Old City, talking to a friend whom I had met only recently. Hetti was a Christian Arab in his twenties who lived in the nearby Armenian quarter. Suddenly he explained that he had to get back home because his parents worried a great deal about his safety, especially at night, in view of the fact that they were living in an occupied country. I asked him what he meant, and he produced a Jordanian passport along with the official 'papers' that he had to show whenever he was stopped by an Israeli patrol.

"As an American Jew I had been taught that Israel was my country—a place where I would always be welcome. What did that make me now? A conqueror? A usurper? It wasn't the last time during the course of that year that I would be forced to retreat into my American-ness and be made to see that no matter how much we think we understand, we are always strangers in a foreign land. I also discovered that there is no substitute for firsthand knowledge and direct experience. Indeed, for the student who goes abroad seeking to know, it soon becomes apparent that the only true classroom is the one out there."

—Frederick G. Levine
Class of 1978
Amherst College
Writer, author of *The Psychic Handbook*
Shutesbury, MA

- "Why are you interested in Lake Forest?" (Lake Forest College—Lake Forest, Illinois)
- "Write about a significant experience or influential person." (Ohio Wesleyan University—Delaware, Ohio)
- "What is your greatest achievement?" (Whitman College—Walla Walla, Washington)
- "Write about an important modern issue." (Hood College—Frederick, Maryland)

- "What are your expectations for college?" (University of Denver—Denver, Colorado)
- "Describe yourself." (Alfred University—Alfred, New York)
- "Do you consider yourself a Christian?" (Gordon College—Wenham, Massachusetts)
- "How do you plan to prepare for your field of study?" (Pratt Institute of Technology—Brooklyn, New York)
- "Choose any topic." (Fisk University—Nashville, Tennessee)
- "Why should you be admitted to Baylor?" (Baylor University—Waco, Texas)

As you can see, essay topics can run the gamut from the general to the specific. The following sample essays show two approaches you can take.

Who Are You?

I call myself an open-minded person. My mother, on the other hand, says that I am "different," whereas politicians might label me as a "liberal."

Look at where I have spent the first seventeen years of my life, and you may wonder how I came to be the way I am. I sometimes wonder myself. I have never had a classmate outside of my own race. I have never had a female minister or doctor. Homosexuality is a taboo topic in my home. Many people from my community think things are fine the way they are, but I do not.

I can think of a few childhood incidents that influenced my thinking; one third-grade memory is especially strong. One day my teacher told us that some scientists tested the intelligence of brown-eyed people and found them to be inferior. As a result, our brown-eyed classmates had to be separated from the rest of us. What was more, the "brown-eyes" were not allowed to play on the merry-go-round or use the same restrooms. This lasted a whole day. On the second day our teacher told us she had made a "terrible mistake": Brown-eyed children were actually smarter than the others. This time the students with blue, green or gray eyes were treated as second-class citizens. Later, the teacher explained that this had all been part of a lesson, and went on to explain. She didn't have to, because I already understood.

Since then, I have worked very hard to be fair to people whether or not they are like me. It is not easy, but I try. I try not to encourage ethnic jokes, to assume that everyone is attracted to the opposite sex or to expect boys to pay for my movie tickets.

I love my home and family but I am ready to stretch my legs. As a student at XYZ University, I can bring a different perspective to your community and take back what I learn to my community. Not only will I be excited about participating in your Residents' Assistant program, I hope to become involved in University theater, too. At the same time, your diverse student population will enable me to learn about all sorts of people and viewpoints. Your strong political science department, the area of study I am most interested in, will show me how people of all backgrounds and nationalities try to work together, and how to cope when they have disagreements. Finally, I want to learn from XYZ if my way of thinking is truly open-minded, different, and liberal, or if it is just another way of thinking.

Why Did You Choose XYZ University and Why Do You Think You Should be Accepted?

I love challenge. Every one-on-one basketball game with my brother is a fight to the end. I get more excited about entering a spelling bee than going on vacation. Fund-raising for the Boy Scouts is more than a job, it's an adventure. I've enjoyed some world-class challenges in my seventeen years, but now I am embarking on my biggest to date: college. I'm nervous, but I have to admit that I think I'm the man for the job.

If I am accepted at XYZ University, I will take advantage of its fine liberal-arts program. I am looking forward to unravelling the mysteries of astronomy, digging for the deeper meanings of Shakespeare, and everything in between. Although I have not chosen my career yet, I feel certain that XYZ will introduce me to an incredible range of possibilities. No matter what I eventually home in on, I know, from what I've read about XYZ and what I've heard from current students that when I graduate I will have "one leg up on the competition." In fact, one of the many reasons why I have chosen XYZ is because it is so highly selective about the students it accepts.

I'm also aware of XYZ's demanding academic requirements. As a high-school student with a B + average and an extra-strong extracurricular record, I feel I am well prepared to handle a demanding work load even as I participate in college groups such as fraternities, intramural sports and perhaps student government. (However, if I have learned anything in high school it's that activities must be limited or classwork suffers. I plan to put this lesson to good use at XYZ.)

If I can meet the challenges that XYZ offers me, I'll be better prepared to meet the hundreds of other contests that lie ahead of me in the years after college. Already, I feel as if I am one step closer: I have written an essay that challenged my wits and my temper but that finally earned my personal approval. I hope it earns yours.

These essays are different, but they are similar in a few ways. Both are vehicles for telling readers something significant about the writer. Both stick to the point. And both conclude with a tidy, ambitious, upbeat ending.

The first example follows English-rule form. The first sentence, "I call myself an open-minded person," isn't exciting but it is safe. It introduces you to the topic, exactly what a topic sentence is supposed to do. The rest of the sentences in this paragraph set the tone for the rest of the essay; it's an effective introduction.

The next three paragraphs comprise the body of the essay. Note how the first sentence in each of these paragraphs introduces you to the topic of the paragraph. Further, each paragraph has a point. Point 1, for example, is about the author's past: "Look where I have spent the first seventeen years of my life." Point 2 is a specific "third-grade memory," a lesson that the writer learned. And Point 3 is the author's evaluation of the lesson. The final paragraph, or conclusion, sums up the essay even as it adds a thought.

See how each point relates to the next one, and how they lead you through the story? The author even throws in a "story" to illustrate the essay and give it color.

In the second essay the author chose everyday language, instead of perfectly structured sentences. At the same time, he took pains not to misspell any words, leave any prepositions dangling at the end of sentences or begin sentences with a conjunction.

What style should you choose for your essay? That depends on the school, the question and you. A "liberal" topic or offbeat style, for example, might not be the right choice for a staunchly conservative school. On the other hand, an offbeat essay question calls for something more than a straight-and-narrow, less-than-creative answer.

When you write your essays, remember that the goal is to tell admissions officers about yourself—something more than the straight facts which appear on your application or in your transcript. Choose a topic appropriate to the essay question and to the business of college, but strive for honesty and freshness. Admissions officers read ninety-nine essays a day (and maybe more!), so give them something to remember you by.

There are plenty of books on essay-writing. Barron's *Write Your Way into College* is one of the best. But be forewarned: These books are so full of dos and don'ts, you're likely to throw up your hands and surrender. Don't. Just read the advice, think about it and then put the book aside. You can return to it for review as needed.

When you've decided actually to write your essay, don't just sit down and whip it off in an hour or less. Think about the question and how you want to handle it. Try to outline your

---

CAMPUS BOUND! APPLICATION LOG

College	Application due
1.	
2.	
3.	
4.	
5.	
Example State U.	2/15

thoughts, the way you do for school reports. Write, rewrite, edit and, if necessary, wad up your efforts in a little ball and start over. It goes without saying that you should check your grammar and spelling if you're not 110 percent sure. You might even want your English teacher to take a look at your work. Resist the temptation to try and craft one generic essay which will work for the varied essays you'll be asked to write; you'll end up either not answering the question, not saying very much, or both. To end on a positive note, remember: You're going to have to write essays and sell yourself a whole lot more in the coming years; master the skill now and you've mastered it forever!

WHEN THE VERDICTS COME IN

Nervous? Try not to be. Keep this encouraging fact in mind: About 75 percent of college students are admitted to their first-choice schools.

Once you've mailed your applications and made sure that all letters, transcripts and other paper work have been taken care of, all you can do is sit back and wait. The results usually roll in

---

CAMPUS BOUND! APPLICATION LOG (continued)

Application sent	Transcript sent	Test Scores sent
2/1	2/1	ACT SAT

during April. If a college's reply seems to be very late, it's okay to call the admissions office to make sure everything is under control.

In the meantime, if you get any "missing information" postcards from your colleges, don't panic. There's probably a good explanation. For example, some high schools send all their transcripts to colleges at one time, so yours may arrive later than your application. Or perhaps your teacher got a late start on her letter of recommendation. If you receive such a postcard, just check with the appropriate office or person to be sure your wires aren't crossed.

How to handle the waiting period between due dates and notification letters? Keep busy. In the flurry of completing your applications, you may have fallen behind on your high-school work. Now is a good time to bury yourself in the books. Lay the groundwork for a strong finish—you're not going to feel like catching up at graduation time.

Keep a low profile among your friends, too, when it comes to talking about college. That way, if you're actually accepted to the college of your dreams, you'll have some wonderful news. On the other hand, if you've been talking up your choices—but you aren't accepted—you're bound to feel embarrassed. Above all,

---

CAMPUS BOUND! APPLICATION LOG (continued)

Letters requested	Financial aid forms sent	Notification received
1.		
2.		
3.		
4.		
5.		

12/20 Ms. Edwards   FAF 3/1   Accepted 4/2

1/10 Coach Jordan   School's 2/1

be good to yourself. If you followed all the steps in choosing your colleges and did your best on your applications, you deserve a medal. This is serious stuff, but there comes a time when you have to throw up your hands and let fate (admissions officers) decide. So take a break and treat yourself to some R&R while you wait—you've earned it.

How the Selection Process Works

Generally speaking, large public institutions take fewer variables into consideration, whereas smaller private schools delve further into your accomplishments and character. Even so, it's safe to say that all admissions officers look at your high school grade-point average and class rank in conjunction with your test scores first. All the other stuff—essays, recommendations, honors, interviews—are important, but carry less clout.

The majority of colleges distribute the applications they receive to admissions officers, who separate them into three piles: "great," "average" and "questionable." The great ones (who have the most impressive GPAs and test scores) are most likely to get in. When it comes to the average candidates, officers will take a closer look at the secondary qualities, such as

---

CAMPUS BOUND! APPLICATION LOG (continued)

Acceptance/ denial sent	Fees or other forms sent
Acceptance 4/10	Housing $50 5/5
	Health Info 5/5

extracurricular activities and the essay. The questionable candidates are subject to the greatest amount of scrutiny. Their applications are either tossed out of the running or discussed by a committee.

That's the basic system, but of course, every college has different standards and procedures. Schools with a liberal admissions policy are most concerned with GPA and test score minimums; once candidates qualify, they are accepted on a first-come, first-served basis.

The standards of highly selective colleges are less cut-and-dried. Once your application meets the academic criteria, the admissions staff will judge your ability to succeed in the college and in the program of your choice. If you want to major in music, for example, they will look at your extracurricular activities (e.g. band practice) in relation to music. Admissions officers will also weigh your ability to accommodate any slots they're trying to fill. For example, let's say XYZ University has a goal to include more tap-dancers, redheads and North Dakota natives in its student body. If you fit into any of these groups, your chances of succeeding at XYZ University may be better. Yes, it's vague, confusing and extremely subjective, but the admissions officers at highly selective schools believe their selection process is the only way to maintain quality.

How to Handle Rejection

Because there are so many variables in this entire process, we as individuals can have only so much control over the results. You're no stranger to this fact of life—haven't you lost contests or awards that you felt you deserved? The same thing happens after college, whether you're competing for a job, for example.

So when you learn you've been denied acceptance to a college, take it easy on yourself. You may very well have been underqualified, or you may have missed out by a hair. What's important is that you tried, and that admissions officers aren't out to hurt you. It's extremely hard to judge a student's aptitude without knowing him or her, but it has to be done. Some of the ways this is done may strike you as unfair or incomplete, especially if you feel you've been judged negatively. It hurts, but we all have to lose sometimes. When you get through this, you'll feel a little stronger and you'll appreciate your victories even more.

If you have missed out by a hair, say because you are short one language or math requirement, your denial letter will often specify this as the reason. It doesn't hurt to call and discuss this with the admissions office. Often they will let you take the class in summer school so you can be accepted.

Now let's turn our attention to the colleges that do want you. If you followed the strategies on page 130, you'll have at least one. Choose the one that you like the best and be proud to attend a college that is proud to have you.

WORDS OF WISDOM

"What happens if you choose the college, but the college does not choose you . . . ? You cannot place in the hand of an admissions officer something so valuable as your heart. You are what you are, and you are not greater if you get into your first-choice school or less if you do not. You will make the best of life's opportunities and your own gifts—if you believe in yourself."

—Jacob Neusner
How to Grade Your Professors and Other Unexpected Advice

No Acceptances?

Did something go wrong? If you disagree with the decision, you or your guidance counselor can call the admissions office to ask for reasons. You may not get the answer you want to hear, but at least you can find out if there was any misunderstanding and perhaps rectify the situation. Otherwise, it's time for Plan B.

• Ask your guidance counselor for a list of schools that will accept applications in April. Your best bets are public schools or the less-selective private colleges. Find out under what circumstances you can apply late: Do you forgo housing and financial aid? Do you promise to accept? Do you begin in the summer quarter?

• Enroll in a community college and improve upon your weaknesses. If poor math and science grades are the culprits, then work hard to improve your credentials. A semester or year from now, when you reapply to the colleges that turned you down, you'll look a lot better. In fact, you'll get extra points for determination. (Do check with the colleges in question before trying this strategy, though, to make sure it meets with their approval.)

• A few schools have "appeal" programs. Find out if—and how—your college reevaluates denials and proceed accordingly.

Waiting in Line

Maybe you're relieved to hear that you made the waiting list. After all, it's better than an outright rejection. But in some ways, waiting lists are even tougher to handle than denials.

That's because waiting lists put you in limbo—you're not in and you're not out. The college may legitimately plan to squeeze you into the next available spot once the first batch of students decline the invitation. Or the college may be playing politics, with no real intention of accepting you (instead of turning down a senator's son, for instance, some administrators would rather put him on the waiting list). In the meantime, you're stuck until you're given the sign. You can't accept any other schools, nor can you put them off.

Or can you? According to the National Association of College Admissions Counselors, you have the right to wait until all your college choices have replied or until May 1 (whichever comes first) until you're required to make your final decisions. So that buys you a little time.

What if it's May 1 and you still haven't been taken off a waiting list? First, call the admissions office to be sure your name hasn't fallen into a black hole. If you're still on the list, you'll have to make a decision. Can you give up this school in favor of another college? Keep in mind that you can't be sure you'll get in, and the verdict may arrive as late as August. Or do

According to *Peterson's National College Databank*, these are the most "selective" schools in the country:

Amherst College—Amherst, Massachusetts
Bowdoin College—Brunswick, Maine
Brown University—Providence, Rhode Island
California Institute of Technology—Pasadena, California
Columbia College—New York City, New York
Cornell University—Ithaca, New York
Dartmouth College—Hanover, New Hampshire
Duke University—Durham, North Carolina
Georgetown University—Washington, D.C.
Harvard University—Cambridge, Massachusetts
Harvey Mudd College—Claremont, California
Haverford College—Haverford, Pennsylvania
Massachusetts Institute of Technology—Cambridge, Massachusetts
Pomona College—Claremont, California
Princeton University—Princeton, New Jersey
Rice University—Houston, Texas
Stanford University—Stanford, California
Swarthmore College—Swarthmore, Pennsylvania
United States Air Force Academy—Colorado Springs, Colorado
United States Coast Guard Academy—New London, Connecticut
United States Merchant Marine Academy—Kings Point, New York
United States Military Academy—West Point, New York
United States Naval Academy—Annapolis, Maryland
Wesleyan University—Middletown, Connecticut
Williams College—Williamstown, Massachusetts
Yale University—New Haven, Connecticut

you have to take a chance at gaining admission to this particular college? If so, you've got your work cut out for you.

First, send back the acceptance card with a deposit to one of the colleges that made you a firm invitation. You don't want to make this move lightly—and you don't ever want to accept more than one college at a time. Some institutions compare notes, and they don't take kindly to students who occupy more than one space. However, if you're fully prepared to attend the school you actually accept, it's okay to back out if and when you're admitted to your first-choice college. (You'll probably lose your deposit, though.)

Then get your counselor to find out just what your status is. Do you really have a chance, or are there 1,500 other kids in front of you? Is there anything you can do to improve the odds? If the admissions office's reaction to your inquiry is positive, go for broke. Rewrite your essay, if need be. Get your alumna aunt to write a letter on your behalf. Schedule a personal interview to persuade the admissions office to accept you. Make it clear that you will definitely attend the school once you gain admission. Don't worry about overdoing your enthusiasm. Apparently, this is what college administrators expect. Determination wins.

Joy to the World

So you're one of those lucky devils who gets accepted by more than one college? And you thought you weren't going to have to make any more decisions? Well, which will it be? How about the one that looks best on a sweatshirt? Or the school that gives you the longest summer vacation?

Seriously, if you're in yet another dilemma, let the financial-aid packages be the best determinant. A couple of weeks or so after your letter of acceptance arrives, you'll hear from the financial-aid office. Compare the offers from the various schools. Keep in mind that grants and scholarships are preferable to long-term loans.

And, of course, you'll weigh the financial picture with all the other things that attracted you to the colleges in the first place. Go back for a visit, if you're still not sure. Ask more questions. Then, if the answer isn't clear, go with your gut instinct. If you'd like to stay near home but you know in your heart you can't pass up Pepperdine, then you know what you have to do. Sorry, but you're on your own.

Once you decide, carry through. Notify the college of your acceptance and immediately decline the other schools. Somebody, somewhere, would like to have your spot. In time, your college will contact you with information about the year ahead as well as requests for information about you. Respond promptly. And don't trouble yourself with wondering about what might have been. You have chosen your college—and chosen it well. Get on with your senior year and get geared up for fall.

SO YOU WON'T BE SURPRISED

Congratulations! It feels great to know where you're going to be next year, doesn't it? You're going to have fun these last weeks— attending your final high-school functions, celebrating graduation and thinking about what college will be like. But don't forget to keep up the good work. After all, it got you this far. Although you probably won't damage your grades and jeopardize graduation at this late date, there's no sense in taking chances. Have a good time, but don't mess up all that you've worked for.

In the Meantime
What do you have to do between now and September?

☐ Comply with your college's requests. You may have to chose your dormitory, send money, provide health information and so on.

☐ Get a summer job. Remember that most colleges expect you to contribute a part of your education costs. And besides, who couldn't use some extra spending money?

☐ Plan on attending your college's orientation session. Many colleges invite freshmen and their parents to the campus during the summer.

SURVEY SAYS:

How is college different from what you expected?

"The teachers. They don't spoon-feed you like they do in high school. They just tell you general information, and then, if you want to know more, you have to dig it out. I really have to apply myself more than I thought I would."

—Wes Vaughn
East Tennessee State University
Johnson City, Tennessee

"The size of the classes. Some of them—especially in the first two years—have 500 or 600 students. In high school the teacher knows you and there's more interaction. But in a large college class you just sort of sit there and take notes. You don't get individualized attention and help."

—Stacey Collins
University of Maryland
College Park, Maryland

"I used to go to Mount Holyoke in South Hadley, Massachusetts, and I was surprised by the professors. I didn't expect them to help us, but I found out they really cared. They even went to dinner with us and talked. When I transferred to the University of Colorado, I was told that the professors were 'available,' but, as it turns out, they're really at a distance. I guess that's the difference between a small college and a large college."

—Sheryl Gofman
University of Colorado
Boulder, Colorado

☐ Scope out the dormitories and find out what you'll need to bring to campus.

☐ Contact your roommate(s). Your college will most likely tell you who she/he is. By calling or writing ahead of time, you'll have made your first new friend and you can plan who's bringing the stereo, who has a coffee maker and so on.

☐ Ask for practical graduation gifts. An iron, coffeepot, towels, posters, reference books—people like to give things they know you can use.

☐ Get your finances in order. Pick up any loan checks at the bank. Decide whether to open a checking account at home or in your college town. Talk to your parents about whether you'll need a credit card. If you're going a long way, consider using traveler's checks to get your money where you're going.

☐ Double-check your health. Your college may require a routine examination, anyway. Decide how you'll get prescriptions refilled when you're away from home. Write down the phone numbers of your doctors for easy reference. Check the status of your health insurance—things might have changed when you turned eighteen.

☐ Make travel arrangements. If you're flying to your new campus, make reservations now (be flexible with your dates and you're likely to get a cheaper fare; ask the reservations agent for options). How will you move your gear? Luggage is limited on airplanes, unless you're prepared to pay extra. Consider having some equipment shipped to campus later.

The space below is for you to list other things you have to accomplish between now and September.

☐
☐
☐
☐
☐
☐
☐
☐
☐
☐
☐

Shopping List
Musts:

☐ Laundry bag
☐ Clothes hangers
☐ Detergent
☐ Towels
☐ Sheets (unless your school offers a linen service)
☐ Pillow (unless your school offers a linen service)
☐ Blanket (unless your school offers a linen service)
☐ Alarm clock
☐ School supplies
☐ Clothes
☐ Personal necessities

☐
☐
☐
☐
☐
☐
☐
☐
☐

Maybes:
- ☐ Stereo
- ☐ Television
- ☐ Computer
- ☐ Cooking equipment
- ☐ Wall hangings
- ☐ Furniture
- ☐ Desk lamp
- ☐ Sports gear
- ☐ Telephone
- ☐ Answering machine
- ☐ Car
- ☐
- ☐
- ☐
- ☐
- ☐
- ☐
- ☐
- ☐
- ☐
- ☐
- ☐
- ☐
- ☐
- ☐
- ☐
- ☐
- ☐
- ☐
- ☐

The Typical Freshman Load

At some point—usually when you attend freshman orientation or otherwise get to the campus—you'll choose your first college courses. As a freshman, you won't have much leeway. In fact, some colleges will tell you what to take. But in most cases, you'll be able to make a few selections among the requirements.

During the first year, your college will probably limit the number of hours you may carry each semester or quarter. Seventeen hours is average for students on a semester system; fifteen is the norm for quarter systems. That's because semesters are longer than quarters.

The number of hours of credit you get per class roughly represents how many hours you'll spend in class each week. A three-hour class, for example, usually meets for an hour each on Monday, Wednesday and Friday. A four-hour class might meet for an hour each on Tuesday and Thursday in addition to a two-hour lab on any other day. However, don't expect colleges to stick to the rules every time; you may have to attend class two hours to get one hour of credit.

Following are the first quarter/semester loads for Allen and Michele. In Allen's case, freshmen were allowed to take the usual course load for a quarter: about fifteen hours. Although Allen planned to major in business, his particular school, a large state university, did not allow him to declare a major until his sophomore year. Allen consulted the catalog for business-major requirements and chose his courses accordingly. As you can see, they are all general but varied. How did he choose? Allen didn't have to take U.S. history, but he did have to have a certain number of credit hours in history. He didn't have to take astronomy, but he did have to have a certain number of credit hours in the sciences. Look up your major in the catalog to find out what your requirements are.

If Michele is on the semester system, why is she taking the same number of hours as Allen, who is on the quarter system? Because her college requires that freshmen take smaller-than-average loads. In fact, she's taking one hour more than most freshmen, since she's involved in voice class. Michele hasn't declared her major yet, but her small liberal-arts college has core requirements for freshmen, anyway.

Allen's First Quarter

Major: Business (undeclared)

Subject	*# of hours*
English Composition	3
United States History	4
Introductory Astronomy	4
Pre-Calculus	4
Total Hours	15

Michele's First Semester

Major: Undeclared

Subject	*# of hours*
Western Tradition	4
Communications	3
Chemistry and Society	4
Introduction to Music	3
Voice Class I	1
Total Hours	15

What Will It Be Like in the Beginning?

You'll be so busy with the hustle and bustle of moving in, you won't be able to answer this question for a while—you just won't notice. Everything will be new and different: going to a cafeteria to eat instead of sitting down at your mom's dinner table; sharing the bathroom with strangers; staying up late without anyone noticing; goofing off in your dorm room between classes; having a whole bunch of people your age around at all hours of the day. You might feel as if you're at camp or something. It will have that same feeling of "I'm not here for a long time, just a good one."

SURVEY SAYS:
What advice would you offer to
college-bound high-school students?

"If you're undecided about your major—and most people are in the first year—don't go to a small college. Go to a college that has a lot to offer. I know a lot of people who had to transfer from small colleges because the programs they became interested in weren't available. That's why I went to UT—it offers so much I figured I couldn't go wrong."

—Krista Bice
University of Tennessee
Knoxville, Tennessee

"Work as hard as you can from the start. Don't think, 'Oh, I'm just a freshman, I can get away with it.' Get organized and don't put off deadlines. That's when you start to get into trouble, I've noticed. When work piles up it's hard to catch up."

—Marley Majcher
Georgetown University
Washington, D.C.

"First of all, enjoy high school. I go to a school that's pretty tough—the work is ten times harder than high school was. Second of all, work on math and science like crazy, especially if you're in the technical majors like engineering, chemistry or any of the sciences. Get the basics down before you go to college, or you'll be finished."

—Denton Sisk
Virginia Military Institute
Lexington, Virginia

After a week or so, it will sink in that you are there to stay—for a while, anyway. You'll still have fun, but things will start to get a little routine, even annoying. Like eating at the cafeteria. At first you'll enjoy being able to pick out anything you want, anytime you want. You'll love meeting your friends for dinner. But eventually you might get tired of going out in public for every meal and eating the same old stuff. Then, too, your dormitory might be the best on campus, but when it's time to study or sleep you may long for peace and quiet, not the sounds of ceaseless partying. After years of being in school from 8:30 to 3:00, your unstructured college schedule may leave you giddy with variety. Yet along with that free time comes much more work; college courses place great emphasis on the work you do outside the classroom.

This isn't meant to depress you, but to prepare you for the inevitable. College is fun, but hard work picks up where fun leaves off (or vice versa). With that in mind, you'll be ready for the long lines to use the laundry facilities, the thick red tape in the financial-aid office, the boring economics lectures. And you'll appreciate the homecoming parties, the pizza study breaks and the practical jokes all the more.

Typical Programs for the First Two Years

Following is my personal transcript for my freshman and sophomore years at the University of Tennessee at Knoxville. I was a journalism news–editorial major in the College of Communications.

Freshman/Fall Quarter

Course Number	Description	Quarter Hours	Grade
English 1010 [A]	English Composition [B]	3	A [C]
History 1510	Development of Western Civilization I	4	B
Music 3657	Marching Band	1	A
Philosophy 1510	Introductory Philosophy: Human Nature and Values	4	A

Total Quarter Hours: 12
Quarter Grade: 3.75
Cumulative Grade: 3.75

Freshman/Winter Quarter

Course Number	Description	Quarter Hours	Grade
Astronomy 2110	Introductory Astronomy	4	C
English 1020	English Composition [D]	3	A
History 1520	Development of Western Civilization II	4	B
Music 3654	Varsity Band [E]	1	A
Philosophy 1520	Introductory Philosophy: Conscious Reality	4	B

Total Quarter Hours: 16 [F]
Quarter Grade: 3.0 [G]
Cumulative Grade: 3.32 [H]

SUMMER-BEFORE-COLLEGE READING

Just to get you in the right frame of mind, you might want to check out some of the following books:

The Lords of Discipline
Pat Conroy, 1980

A Separate Peace
John Knowles, 1959

End Zone
Don DeLillo, 1972

Love Story
Erich Segal, 1970

Beer in the Snooker Club
Waguih Ghali, 1964

Look Homeward, Angel
Thomas Wolfe, 1929

Freshman/Spring Quarter

Course Number	Description	Quarter Hours	Grade
Astronomy 2120 [I]	Introductory Astronomy	4	B
Communications 1110 [J]	Introduction to Communications	3	B
English 1032	English Composition	3	B
Music 1210 [K]	Orientation in Music I	3	A
Psychology 2500	General Psychology	4	B

Total Quarter Hours: 17
Quarter Grade: 3.18
Cumulative Grade: 3.27

Sophomore/Fall Quarter

Course Number	Description	Quarter Hours	Grade
Geology 1410	General Geology I	4	C
Journalism 2215	Basic News Writing	4	B
Music 3657	Marching Band	1	A
Sociology 1510	General Sociology	4	A
Spanish 2110 [L]	Intermediate Spanish	3	A

Total Quarter Hours: 15
Quarter Grade: 3.25
Cumulative Grade: 3.26

Sophomore/Winter Quarter

Course Number	Description	Quarter Hours	Grade
English 2510	English Masterpieces	4	W^M
Journalism 2220	Reporting	4	B
Music 1220	Orientation in Music II	3	C
Music 3654	Varsity Band	1	A
Political Science 3750	The Urban Polity	4	B
Spanish 2120	Intermediate Spanish	3	B

Total Quarter Hours: 15
Quarter Grade: 2.87
Cumulative Grade: 3.18

Sophomore/Spring Quarter

Course Number	Description	Quarter Hours	Grade
Economics 2110	Introductory Economics	3	C
English 2510	English Masterpieces	4	A
English 3470	Writing Poetry	3	A
Journalism 2230	Editing for Mass Media	3	C
Physical Education 2781^N	Elementary Tennis	2	B

Total Quarter Hours: 15
Quarter Grade: 3.0
Cumulative Grade: 3.10

You'll notice that parts of the transcript have been labeled with letters. The following is a key to understanding what those labels mean.

A: Each course has an official name consisting of the subject and its number. Generally, the 100 or 1000 courses are freshman level, 200 or 2000 courses are sophomore level and so on.

B: After the course name and number, you'll usually find a brief description of the class.

C: The final grade for that course.

D: Three quarters of English Composition are usually required of everyone.

E: I always signed up for Band—both Marching (football) and Varsity (basketball) as if they were regular courses, since our practices had to be scheduled in the early mornings and late afternoons.

F: The number of credit hours I earned that quarter. Because Marching Band took so much time during my first quarter in school, I took a very small load. Unfortunately, I continued to take easy loads, so I had to work extra hard during my last two years to graduate on time.

G: My grade-point average for the quarter. It was never that high again.

H: My grade-point average for the combined quarters. As I got more involved in newspapers and nightlife, my cumulative GPA slid.

I: I hated classes like this, but my major required twelve hours of natural sciences.

J: Notice how we weren't allowed to get down to the business of our major until later. The idea is first to build a general knowledge and, not insignificantly, to weed us out. Journalism and communications classes were overcrowded, and a percentage of students drop out in the first year anyway. By my senior year, I was deep into advanced reporting and communications law.

K: Electives. You might say I chose too many "easy" classes—and sometimes I did—but at the time, I wanted to be (and eventually became) entertainment editor for the college newspaper. These classes not only fleshed out my music background, but they also interested me.

Why I Chose Oxford College and Stetson University
—Atlanta, Georgia and DeLand, Florida

"At 450, the total enrollment at Emory University's Oxford College was smaller than my high-school graduation class in Kingsport, Tennessee. And that's what I wanted; I felt I would be more comfortable at a small college—I wouldn't get lost in the shuffle. I liked Atlanta, too—Oxford is about twenty-five miles away, so it has the advantages of a small community as well as a big city.

"At Oxford, everyone enrolls in a two-year liberal arts program before deciding whether to continue their education at Emory University's Atlanta campus or elsewhere. I thought I would be a math major, but after taking a few 'theoretical calculus' classes I changed my mind. I started leaning toward a business major, but Emory, at that time, didn't have much of a business-school reputation. (Since then, Emory has made significant changes in its business program.) Stetson University, on the other hand, was known for its business school. I also had friends at Stetson, and the fact that it was twenty miles away from Daytona Beach was somewhat appealing. So after completing my associate in arts degree I transferred to Stetson, where I earned a bachelor's degree in business and an MBA.

"My days at Oxford are warm in my memory. I'm still in contact with the friends I made there; even though we're scattered all over the world, we're like one big family. It wasn't quite the same at Stetson and I'm not sure that I needed an MBA. Even so, my education opened some doors—it got me my first job at Georgia Power in Atlanta—and I like what I'm doing today."

—John D. Gregory
Class of 1973 (Oxford)
Class of 1975 (Stetson)
Life Underwriter/Registered Representative
National Life of Vermont Insurance Company
Kingsport, TN

L: I took two years of Spanish in high school but didn't pick it up again until my sophomore year in college. This was a mistake. Because I had waited so long, I was afraid to challenge myself with an advanced class. Consequently, intermediate Spanish was more or less a review. The second mistake: After the winter quarter of my sophomore year, I skipped spring and waited until the fall quarter of my junior year to continue with the course of the next level. I got a C, and it served me right.

M: The "W" means that I withdrew from the class before the cut-off date. My college allowed us a few withdrawals with no penalty toward our grade. I withdrew because I was worried about being overloaded, since I had a new job at a campus cafeteria—scraping plates.

N: I didn't improve my game much, but I got a great tan.

Break a Leg

One thing college students learn in a hurry: They have a license on independence and responsibility. Going to college isn't the same as getting a job and moving out immediately after high school, but it's not the same as being seventeen and living at home, either. In a way, your parents are sending you into the world on a leash. You can make your own decisions about time management and who to hang out with and where to go, but your college and your parents aren't going to let you starve or move in with just anybody or ignore your classes.

Maybe you think you need more responsibility—or less. Look at it this way: You have the chance to break into the real world gradually. Take advantage of it, but don't abuse it. You're bound to make a few mistakes—oversleeping and missing a class, bouncing a check—but use your head and you won't make any major errors. Learn from the little mistakes and be glad that Mom is there to cover your bounced check or that a professor is willing to give you an extension on a deadline. All too soon, you'll be reading up on employment and wondering how four years could have come and gone so swiftly. You'll probably be ready to leave college when the time comes, but enjoy it while you can. These may not be the best years of your life—but they're pretty close.

REFERENCES

The list of resources for college-bound students is long. That's why, on the preceding pages, we didn't always have room enough to provide book titles, addresses and the like, and instead referred you to *References.* Here you are.

Most of the books listed in this section were found in a city library. Keep in mind, though, that since some guides are updated annually your library may not always be up to date. If you're using a guide that *isn't* updated regularly—you can tell by checking the copyright page—you should check with the college to see whether the old information still applies. Current copies are, most likely, available at your local bookstore. However, they do cost money—anywhere from $6.95 to $16.95. Our advice: First see what's available at your school or city library. Then decide whether an investment makes sense.

When you go to the library, look under "Colleges and Universities" in the card catalog. And don't limit yourself to the sources we've listed here; go ahead and sniff around the entire collection to see what else you can turn up. If you're not comfortable with using the library, ask the librarians for help; that's why they're there. In fact, you might as well check with the librarians anyway, since some resources are stored in special sections.

There are other books and services that you can't buy *or* check out—you have to write away for them. Contact these organizations *before* writing away so they can let you know the proper charge for shipping and handling.

Time and time again, you'll come across the college-bound publishing giants: Peterson's, Barron's, Lovejoy's, Arco, Fiske, The College Board. Each of them publishes many, many books covering college in every way, shape and form. Generally speaking, all these names can be trusted. If need be, select them over lesser-known titles.

Finally, your college search depends heavily on a gaggle of addressess, many of which are available here. Feel free to add any others you come across.

General College Guides

Barron's Profiles of American Colleges
Barron's Educational Series, Inc.

The College Handbook
College Board Publications; send $17.95 with the item number (003365) to College Board Publications, Department M39, Box 886, New York, NY 10101-0886.

Comparative Guide to American Colleges
James Cass and Max Birnbaum; Harper & Row Publishers, Inc.

The Fiske Guide to Colleges
Edward B. Fiske; Times Books

Lovejoy's College Guide
Simon & Schuster, Inc.

Peterson's Guide to Four-Year Colleges
Peterson's Guides, Inc.

The Right College
Prentice-Hall Press

Selective or Specialized College Guides

The Black Student's Guide to Colleges
Edited by Barry Beckham; E. P. Dutton

Everywoman's Guide to Colleges and Universities
Edited by Suzanne Howard, Florence Howe and Mary Jo Boehm Strauss;
The Feminist Press

A Guide to Colleges for Learning Disabled Students
Edited by Mary Ann Liscio; Academic Press, Inc.

Insider's Guide to the Colleges
Yale Daily News; St. Martin's Press

Peterson's Guide to Competitive Colleges
Peterson's Guides, Inc.

Peterson's Guide to Two-Year Colleges
Peterson's Guides, Inc.

*The Public Ivys: A Guide to America's Best Public Colleges and
Universities*
Richard Moll; Viking Penguin, Inc.

Selective Guide to the Colleges
Edward Fiske; Times Books

Applications and Interviews

Essays That Worked: 50 Essays from Successful Applications to the Nation's Top Colleges
Edited by Boykin Curry and Brian Kasbar; Mustang Publishing

Write Your Way into College: Composing a Successful Application
George Ehrenhaft; Barron's Educational Series, Inc.

First check the library for the following books. If they're not available, send a check along with the desired item number to: College Board Publications, Department M39, Box 886, New York, NY 10101-0866.

Campus Visits and College Interviews
$9.95; item #002601

The College Admissions Organizer
$16.95; item #002261

Writing Your College Application Essay
$9.95; item #002571

Your College Application
$9.95; item #002474

Tests

Barron's How to Prepare for the SAT
Samuel C. Brownstein, Mitchel Weiner, and Sharon W. Green; Barron's Educational Series, Inc.

Cram Course for the ACT
Suzee J. Vlk; Prentice-Hall Press

Cram Course for the SAT
Robert G. Vlk; Prentice-Hall Press

How to Prepare for Advanced Placement Examinations
Barron's Educational Series, Inc.

How to Prepare for College Entrance Examinations
Brownstein and Weiner, Barron's Educational Series, Inc.

Peterson's SAT Success
Joan Davenport Carris; Peterson's Guides, Inc.

The Princeton Review: Cracking the System, The SAT
Adam Robinson and John Katzman; Villard Books

10 SATs
College Board Publications; send $9.95 and item #003039 to College Board Publications, Department M39, New York, NY 10101-0886.

For information on the SAT, write:
College Entrance Examination Board
888 Seventh Avenue
New York, NY 10019

For information on the ACT, write:
American College Testing Program
Box 168
Iowa City, Iowa 52240

Careers

College to Career
Joyce Slayton Mitchell; send $9.95 for item #002490 to College Board Publications, Department M39, Box 886, New York, NY 10101-0886.

Do What You Love—The Money Will Follow: Discovering Your Right Livelihood
Marsha Sinetar; Paulist Press

The Jobs-Rated Almanac
Les Krantz; Pharos Books; rates jobs on income, work environment, stress and competition levels, security, physical demands and other work-related criteria.

Occupational Outlook Handbook
U.S. Department of Human Services; provides descriptions of careers and their economic forecasts

What Color Is Your Parachute?
Richard Nelson Bolles; Ten Speed Press

Alternatives to College

Careers Without College
Jo Ann Russo; Betterway Publications, Inc.

Offbeat Careers: The Directory of Unusual Work
Al Sacharov; Ten Speed Press

For a free pamphlet about accredited vocational-technical schools, write:
National Association of Trade and Technical Schools
2251 Wisconsin Avenue, NW
Washington, D.C. 20007

Service Academies

For information write:

United States Air Force Academy
Colorado Springs, CO 80840

United States Coast Guard Academy
New London, CT 06320

United States Merchant Marine Academy
Kings Point, NY 10204

United States Military Academy
West Point, New York 10996

United States Naval Academy
Annapolis, MD 21402

Of Special Interest

The Gourman Report: A Rating of Undergraduate Programs in American and International Universities
Dr. Jack Gourman; National Education Standards

Index of Majors
College Board Publications; send $14.95 for item #003373 to College Board Publications, Department M39, Box 886, New York, NY 10101-0886.

The Insider's Guide to Foreign Study: Everything You Need to Know about More Than 430 Academic Adventures Abroad
Benedict A. Leerburger; Addison-Wesley Publishing Co., Inc.

Peterson's National College Databank
Peterson's Guides, Inc.

College Videos

The home-video revolution has made possible the "at-home" college visit. Many colleges offer "video tours" free of charge or for a fee; ask the admissions people for information.

Generally speaking, all of these productions are from five to twenty minutes long, give an overview of what the campus looks like and feature interviews with a variety of students and faculty. Some of the videos are not really videos at all, but consist instead of still images transferred to video format; these are, in truth, no more helpful than brochures or viewbooks. In all cases, you would do well to ask questions of the suppliers before spending any money.

Finally, administrators, counselors and the video producers themselves agree that college videos are helpful during the initial "weeding out" stage of your college search but should not be used as a substitute for visiting a college you are thinking seriously of attending.

These organizations rent or sell college videos:

College Home Videos
1080 North Delaware Avenue
Fourth Floor
Philadelphia, PA 19125
(800) 248-7177

Learning Resources Network
21 West Colony Place
Suite 160
Durham, NC 27705

Videc Inc.
P.O. Box 1287
Franklin, TN 37065
(800) 255-0384

The Info-Disc Corporation offers "College U.S.A." video *laserdiscs*. (These are purchased mostly by high schools but are available to the public as well.)

College U.S.A.
Info-Disc Corporation
4 Professional Drive
Gaithersburg, MD 20879
(301) 926-4300 or (301) 948-2300

The College Board Film Library offers several video presentations, among them "Paying for College," "Your College Application" and "College-Choice, StudentChoice," a guide to the admissions process.

College Board Film Library
c/o West Glen Communications, Inc.
1430 Broadway
New York, N.Y. 10018
(212) 921-2800

College Preparatory Service offers a single two-hour videocassette to be used by students preparing for their SATs. Accompanying the video is a 100-page workbook.

College Preparatory Service
P.O. Box 68068
3300 Monroe Avenue
Rochester, NY 14618-0068
(800) 888-7288

Software

The following college-selection software is intended for home use and is available in IBM, IBM-compatible and Apple formats. Be sure you have the proper computer set-up at home before buying any of the following materials.

"College Explorer"
"College Explorer" was produced by New York City's Logicat using the College Board's *College Handbook* database. Price: $49.95
College Board Publications
Box 886
New York, NY 10101-0886
(212) 713-8000

"Perfect College"
Price: $19.95
Mindscape
3444 Dundee Road
Northbrook, IL 60062
(312) 480-1948 or (312) 480-8715

The college-selection software offered by Peterson's is purchased mostly by high schools, libraries and career centers. (Price: $159 for the four-year-college database and $109 for the two-year-college database.) The Peterson databases are also available through several on-line networks: CompuServe, Bibliographic Retrieval Service (BRS), DIALOG and Dow Jones News/Retrieval Service. Peterson's also has software for SAT preparation, financial-aid calculation and career planning. For information on all of Peterson's software and electronic services, call (800) EDU-DATA.

Other software for students to use when preparing for the PSAT and SAT includes:

"Barron's Computer Study
Program for the SAT"
Price: $49.95
Barron's Educational Series
250 Wireless Boulevard
Hauppauge, NY 11788
(800) 257-5729 in New York State
(800) 645-3476 elsewhere

"SAT Complete"
Price: $39.95
Spinnaker Software
One Kendall Square
Cambridge, MA 02139
(800) 826-0706

"Computer Study Guide for the SAT"
Price: $39.95 IBM, $34.95 Apple
Simon & Schuster
200 Old Tappan Road
Old Tappan, NJ 07675
(201) 767-5937

Miscellaneous

For information about college fairs and your rights as an applicant, write:

National Association of College Administration Counselors
1800 Diagonal Road
Suite 430
Alexandria, VA 22314

Financial Aid

After Scholarships, What?
Peterson's Guides, Inc.

The Best Buys in College Education
Edward B. Fiske; Times Books

College Money Handbook
Peterson's Guides, Inc.

Directory of Financial Aid for Minorities
Gail Ann Schlacter; Reference Service Press

Directory of Financial Aid for Women
Gail Ann Schlacter; Reference Service Press

Peterson's How the Military Will Help You Pay for College
Don M. Betterton; Peterson's Guides, Inc.

Winning Money for College
Alan Deutschmann; Peterson's Guides, Inc.

Check the library or write to College Board Publications (Department #M39, Box 886, New York, NY 10101-0886) for the following books:
The College Cost Book
$13.95; item #003381

How to Pay for Your Children's College Education
Gerald Krefetz; $12.95; item #002482

Check the library or write to Octameron Associates (P.O. Box 3437, Alexandria, VA 22302, 703-823-1882) for information on how to receive the following books:

College Grants from Uncle Sam: Am I Eligible and for How Much?
$2.50

College Loans from Uncle Sam: The Borrower's Guide That Explains It All
$2.50

Earn & Learn: Cooperative Education Opportunities with the Federal Government
$3.00

For information about federal student aid in general, call:
Federal Student Aid Information Center
(800) 353-INFO
Monday through Friday
9 A.M. to 5:30 P.M. (EST)

For information about the Family Financial Statement (FFS), write:
ACT Student Need Analysis Services
P.O. Box 4006
Iowa City, IA 52243

For information about the Financial Aid Form (FAF), write:
College Scholarship Service
CN 6300
Princeton, NJ 08541

For information about state financial aid (the fifty states plus the District of Columbia follow below in alphabetical order), write:

Alabama
Alabama Commission on Higher Education
1 Court Square, Suite 221
Montgomery, AL 36197-0001

Alaska
Alaska Commission on Postsecondary Education
400 Willoughby Avenue
Box FP
Juneau, AK 99811

Arizona
Commision for Postsecondary Education
3030 North Central Avenue
Suite 1407
Phoenix, AZ 85012

Arkansas
Department of Higher Education
1220 West 3rd Street
Little Rock, AR 72201

California
P.O. Box 942845
Sacramento, CA 94245-0845

Colorado
Colorado Commission on Higher Education
Colorado Heritage Center
1300 Broadway, 2nd Floor
Denver, CO 80203

Connecticut
Connecticut Department of Higher Education
61 Woodland Station
Hartford, CT 06105-2391

Delaware
Delaware Higher Education Loan Program
Carvel State Office Building
820 North French Street
4th Floor
Wilmington, DE 19801

District of Columbia
Office of Postsecondary Education Research and Assistance
D.C. Department of Human Services
1331 H Street, N.W.
Suite 600
Washington, D.C. 20005

Florida
Office of Student Financial Assistance
Department of Education
Knott Building
Tallahassee, FL 32399

Georgia
Georgia Student Finance Commission
2082 East Exchange Place
Suite 200
Tucker, GA 30084

Hawaii
State Postsecondary Education Commission
209 Bachman Hall
University of Hawaii
2444 Dole Street
Honolulu, HI 96822

Idaho
Office of State Board of Education
650 West State Street
Room 307
Boise, ID 83720

Illinois
Illinois State Scholarship Commission
106 Wilmot Road
Deerfield, IL 60015

Indiana
State Student Assistance Commission of Indiana
964 North Pennsylvania Street
Indianapolis, IN 46204

Iowa
Iowa College Aid Commission
201 Jewett Building
9th and Grand Avenue
Des Moines, IA 50309

Kansas
Kansas Board of Regents
Suite 609, Capitol Tower
400 SW 8th
Topeka, KS 66603

Kentucky
Kentucky Higher Education Assistance Authority
1050 U.S. 127 South
Frankfort, KY 40601

Louisiana
Governor's Special Commission on Education Services
P.O. Box 44127
Capitol Station
Baton Rouge, LA 70804

Maine
Maine Department of Educational And Cultural Services
Division of Higher Education Services
State House Station 119
Augusta, ME 04333

Maryland
Maryland State Scholarship Board
21000 Guilford Avenue
2nd Floor, Room 207
Baltimore, MD 21218

Massachusetts
The Board of Regents of Higher Education Scholarship Office
150 Causeway Street
Room 600
Boston, MA 02114

Michigan
Michigan Department of Education
P.O. Box 30008
Lansing, MI 48909

Minnesota
Minnesota Higher Education Coordinating Board
Capitol Square, Suite 400
550 Cedar Street
St. Paul, MN 55101

Mississippi
Mississippi Postsecondary Education Financial Assistance Board
P.O. Box 2336
Jackson, MS 39225-2336

Missouri
Coordinating Board for Higher Education
P.O. Box 1438
Jefferson City, MO 65102

Montana
Montana University System
33 South Last Chance Gulch
Helena , MT 59620-3104

Nebraska
Nebraska Coordinating Commission for Postsecondary Education
P.O. Box 95005
Lincoln, NE 68509-5005

Nevada
Student Services
Student Financial Aid Services
University of Nevada at Reno
Room 200 TSSC
Reno, NV 89557-0072

New Hampshire
New Hampshire Postsecondary Education Commission
2½ Beacon Street
Concord, NH 03301

New Jersey
Department of Higher Education
Office of Student Assistance
4 Quakerbridge Plaza
C.N. 540
Trenton, NJ 08625

New Mexico
Commission on Higher Education
1068 Cerrillos Road
Santa Fe, NM 87501-4295

New York
New York State Higher Education Services Corporation
99 Washington Avenue
Albany, NY 12255

North Carolina
North Carolina State Education Assistance Authority
P.O. Box 2688
Chapel Hill, NC 27515-2688

North Dakota
North Dakota Student Financial Assistance Program
10th Floor, State Capitol
Bismarck, ND 58505-0154

Ohio
Ohio Board of Regents
Student Assistance Office
3600 State Office Tower
30 East Broad Street
Columbus, OH 43216

Oklahoma
Oklahoma State Regents for Higher Education
State Capitol Complex
Oklahoma City, OK 73105

Oregon
Oregon State Scholarship Commission
1445 Willamette Street
Eugene, OR 97401

Pennsylvania
Pennsylvania Higher Education Assistance Agency
660 Boas Street
Harrisburg, PA 17102

Rhode Island
Rhode Island Higher Education Assistance Authority
560 Jefferson Boulevard
Warwick, RI 02886

South Carolina
Higher Education Tuition Grants Agency
411 Keenan Building
Box 12159
Columbia, SC 29211

South Dakota
Department of Education and Cultural Affairs
Richard F. Kneip Building
700 Governors Drive
Pierre, SD 57501-2293

Tennessee
Tennessee Student Assistance Corporation
400 James Robertson Parkway
Suite 1950, Parkway Tower
Nashville, TN 37219-5097

Texas
Texas Higher Education Coordinating Board
Texas College and University System
P.O. Box 12788
Austin, TX 78711

Utah
Utah State Board of Regents
3 Triad Center, Suite 550
355 West North Temple
Salt Lake City, UT 84180-1205

Vermont
Vermont Student Assistance Corporation
Champlain Mill
P.O. Box 2000
Winooski, VT 05404-2000

Virginia
State Council of Higher Education for Virginia
James Monroe Building
101 North 14th Street
Richmond, VA 23219

Washington
Financial Aid Office
Higher Education Coordinating Board
908 East Fifth Avenue
Olympia, WA 98504

West Virginia
West Virginia Board of Regents
P.O. Box 4007
Charleston, WV 25364

Wisconsin
Wisconsin Higher Educational Aids Board
P.O. Box 7885
Madison, WI 53707

Wyoming
Wyoming Community College Commission
2301 Central Avenue
Barrett Building, 3rd floor
Cheyenne, WY 82002

INDEX

ABOUT THE AUTHOR

Annette Spence is author of *The Encyclopedia of Good Health,* a six-volume series for junior-high-school students, and a number of other books. Her articles have appeared in *Redbook, Cosmopolitan, Bride's, Weight Watchers* and *Sports Inc.* She graduated in 1983 with a journalism degree from the University of Tennessee, the college of her choice.